CUTTING EDGE

THIRD EDITION

PRE-INTERMEDIATE

WORKBOOK

WITH KEY

SARAH CUNNINGHAM PETER MOOR
AND ANTHONY COSGROVE

CONTENTS

Vocabulary
Leisure activities

1a Complete the phrases with the verbs in the box.

play (x3)   use   watch (x2)   listen (x2)   go (x4)

1 _play_ sport
2 _____ TV
3 _____ to music
4 _____ live music
5 _____ to the gym
6 _____ to the radio
7 _____ the internet
8 _____ to the cinema
9 _____ out with friends
10 _____ computer games
11 _____ a musical instrument
12 _____ to evening classes

b Complete the sentences with the correct form of the verbs in exercise a.

1 My sister always _goes_ out with friends on Saturdays.
2 Do you _____ a musical instrument?
3 I _____ the internet every day at work.
4 Do you _____ to the gym every day?
5 She doesn't _____ TV because she doesn't have much time.
6 My dad _____ to evening classes on Tuesdays. He's learning to dance!
7 Jon _____ computer games every day.
8 I often _____ to the radio in the car.
9 Why don't you ever _____ sport?
10 He _____ to lots of music, like jazz and rock.
11 Do you often _____ live music?
12 They _____ to the cinema on Saturdays.

Grammar focus 1
Revision of questions

2 Complete the questions about Parcheesi, the national game of India, with the question words in the box.

~~what kind~~   how   how long   where   which   who   why   how many   what   when

Parcheesi! The national game of India

1 A: _What kind_ of game is Parcheesi?
   B: It's a board game – like chess or backgammon.
2 A: _____ country does it come from originally?
   B: India.
3 A: _____ do people play it now?
   B: All over the world – it's very popular in the USA.
4 A: _____ does 'Parcheesi' mean?
   B: It comes from 'pacis', which means 25.
5 A: _____ did people start playing it?
   B: Hundreds of years ago. But it only came to Europe in the 19th century.
6 A: _____ invented it?
   B: Nobody knows!
7 A: _____ people can play?
   B: Four.
8 A: _____ do you play?
   B: By moving all your pieces to the centre of the board.
9 A: _____ does a game last?
   B: Usually about half an hour.
10 A: _____ is it so popular?
   B: Because it's easy to learn ... but difficult to play well!

3a Michael Aarons, World 100 metres Champion, is in Rome for an important athletics meeting. Put the words in the correct order to make the journalists' questions.

1 first time / this / Is / here in Rome / your?
   Is this your first time here in Rome?
   No, I first came here about eight years ago.
2 your family / with / here / Is / you?
   _____
   My wife is here; my children are with their
   grandparents in the United States.
3 enjoy / wife / Does / athletics / your?
   _____
   She says so, but I think she's really here because she
   likes shopping!
4 life / you / here in Italy / like / Do?
   _____
   Of course, especially the food and the sunshine!
5 you / about / the Italian champion, Giacomo
   Zanetti / Are / worried?
   _____
   Giacomo is a great athlete and a good friend ... but I
   think I can win!
6 you / Do / have / for young athletes / any advice?
   _____
   Sure. Train hard, live a healthy life and you can be a
   champion, too!

b 🎧 1.1 **Listen and check.**

4a Complete questions 1–6 with one word in each gap.

1 _What_ time is it?
2 How _____ CDs have you got?
3 _____ do you live?
4 _____ often do you play tennis?
5 How _____ does each lesson last?
6 _____ do you live with?

b Match the answers with the questions in exercise a.

a In London.   [3]
b My parents and my two sisters.   [ ]
c Three times a week.   [ ]
d 4 o'clock.   [ ]
e A lot!   [ ]
f 45 minutes.   [ ]

Pronunciation
Stress in questions

5a Read the questions. Which words should be stressed? Choose a or b.

1 ⓐ **What's** your favourite **programme**?
   b What's **your favourite** programme?
2 a Why **do** you like **it**?
   b **Why** do you **like** it?
3 a **How many TVs** do you **have**?
   b **How** many TVs **do** you have?
4 a **Who** do you **watch TV with**?
   b Who **do** you **watch** TV with?
5 a **How long** do you **watch TV every day**?
   b **How** long do you watch TV every **day**?
6 a What **kind of** programmes do you never **watch**?
   b **What kind** of **programmes** do you **never** watch?

b 🎧 1.2 **Listen and check.**

Listen and read
TV classics

6a ∩∩ 1.3 Read and listen to the text about TV classics.

TV classics

What are the most popular TV programmes in your country? Here are five classic TV programmes which are famous in many parts of the world.

Baywatch

Internationally, *Baywatch* is the most popular TV show in history. *Baywatch* has appeared in 148 countries in every continent (except Antarctica!), which means that about one half of the world's population has seen it at some time. From its first episode in 1989, this TV drama had everything: beautiful young men and women in swimming costumes, fantastic sunshine and perfect California beaches. And it wasn't just men who liked it. 65 percent of the people watching it were female.

Walking with Dinosaurs

Walking with Dinosaurs first appeared on British television in 1999. Using modern computer technology, it showed dinosaurs walking, eating, sleeping and fighting 65 million years before TV! The series cost £6 million and it took three years to make. Some scientists said that the programme invented facts about how the dinosaurs lived, but that wasn't a problem for the millions of people who watched it. When it appeared on The Discovery Channel, it became the most popular documentary programme ever on cable TV. The series has appeared in more than 90 countries and has been so successful that a 3D film version is being made.

Fawlty Towers

In this classic British comedy of the 1970s, John Cleese plays Basil Fawlty, the owner of a hotel in a small town by the sea. Basil is always angry: angry with his wife, Sybil, angry with the people who work in his hotel (including Manuel, the waiter from Spain) and even angry with the hotel guests. The last episode of *Fawlty Towers* appeared more than 30 years ago, but you can still see this classic British comedy all over the world.

Big Brother

Some people loved it, some people hated it, but one thing is certain: *Big Brother*, the world's first reality TV show, changed TV for ever. What happens when you put a group of young men and women in a house together and allow them no contact with the world outside? And what happens if they are on television 24 hours a day? A Dutchman called John de Mol had the original idea, and the first *Big Brother* appeared on TV in the Netherlands in 1999. More than 40 countries have had their own *Big Brother*s since then.

Pop Idol

In 2001, British music boss Simon Fuller had the idea of a TV 'talent show' for members of the public who wanted to be pop singers. Thousands of singers, good and bad, appeared in front of three judges and TV viewers could vote for the best ten by telephone, text message or over the internet. The idea was a big success internationally and the United States soon had its own *American Idol*. Similar shows appeared all over the world, from Russia to the Arab world. Diana Karazon, 19, from Jordan, won the first Arab *Super Star* in August 2004. Also in 2004, Simon Cowell created another TV talent show called *The X Factor*, which replaced *Pop Idol*, and this became even more popular around the world.

b Read the text again and complete the information below with a name or number.

1 the number of countries where *Baywatch* has appeared

_148_

2 the year *Baywatch* first appeared on TV

3 the number of years it took to make *Walking with Dinosaurs*

4 the number of countries where *Walking with Dinosaurs* has appeared

5 the name of the most important character in *Fawlty Towers*

6 when the last episode of *Fawlty Towers* appeared

7 the person who had the original idea for *Big Brother*

8 when *Big Brother* first appeared on Dutch TV

9 the person who had the original idea for *Pop Idol*

10 the winner of *Super Star* in 2004

Vocabulary
Sports and games

7a Complete the words by adding the missing vowels.

1 b_a_ll
2 equ_pment
3 pl_yer
4 w_nner

5 k_ck
6 te_m
7 sc_re
8 thr_w

b Complete the text with the correct form of the words in exercise a.

Football

You don't need much ¹_____ to play football. You only really need a ²_____ and a place to play. Two ³_____ play a game of football and each team usually has eleven ⁴_____ . They ⁵_____ the ball with their feet and can only use their hands to ⁶_____ the ball if it's gone off the pitch. They try to put the ball into a net and when they do this, they ⁷_____ a goal. The team with the most goals is the ⁸_____ of the match.

Grammar focus 2
Present simple and frequency phrases

8a Read the text about the Wilson sisters.

The Wilson Sisters

Jennifer and Rosemary Wilson are twin sisters and they're both famous. But they have very different lives!

Jennifer lives in London. She's a well-known TV presenter and she gets up at 3 a.m. every day to introduce the popular breakfast TV show *Good Morning, UK!* She finishes work at about 10:30 a.m.
Rosemary is a professional tennis player. She now lives in Beverly Hills, USA with her American husband, Ron. Rosemary comes to England two or three times a year to play. She always stays with her sister.

b Correct the sentences about the Wilson sisters.

1 Jennifer and Rosemary have very similar lives.
   They don't have very similar lives. They have very different lives.

2 Jennifer and Rosemary live in the same country.

3 Jennifer lives in Beverly Hills.

4 She works in the evening.

5 Rosemary plays golf.

6 She lives with her mother.

7 She stays in a hotel when she comes to England.

8 Jennifer and Rosemary see each other every weekend.

c **Write the questions for the answers below.**

1 *Where does Jennifer Wilson live?*
She lives in London.
2 _____
At 3 a.m.
3 _____
At about 10:30 a.m.
4 _____
In Beverly Hills.
5 _____
Two or three times a year.
6 _____
To play tennis.
7 _____
With her sister.

d 🎧 1.4 **Listen and check. Practise saying the questions.**

9a **Read about John's family. Put the phrases in the correct order to make a text.**

a meals together and at meals we usually ☐

b us and they love sports, too. My grandfather ☐

c talk about sports. My grandparents often visit ☐

d I come from a really sporty family. We always eat ☐ 1

e to the gym in the morning before breakfast. We ☐

f we never watch sport on TV because we're too busy! ☐

g occasionally go to a football match together, which is fun. But ☐

h often plays tennis and he's 70. And my grandmother usually goes ☐

b 🎧 1.5 **Listen and check.**

10 **Replace the phrase in bold with a frequency phrase. Use the word in brackets to help you.**

1 I go to English lessons **on Tuesdays and Thursdays**.
I go to English lessons ___*twice a week*___ . (week)

2 We usually go on holiday **in April, in July and in December**.
We usually go on holiday _____ . (year)

3 We go swimming **every Sunday**.
We go swimming _____ . (week)

4 It's important to visit the dentist **every six months**.
It's important to visit the dentist _____ . (year)

5 My friend goes running **on Mondays, Wednesdays, Fridays and Sundays**.
My friend goes running _____ . (week)

6 I check my email **in the morning and in the evening**.
I check my email _____ . (day)

7 I go to visit my cousin in Madrid about **every four weeks**.
I go to visit my cousin in Madrid about _____ . (month)

8 She washes her hair **on Mondays, Wednesdays and Saturdays**.
She washes her hair _____ . (week)

9 He sees his doctor **every 15 days**.
He sees his doctor _____ . (month)

10 I go to the gym at 7 a.m. **on Monday, Tuesday, Wednesday, Thursday, Friday, Saturday and Sunday**.
I go to the gym at 7 a.m. _____ . (day)

Grammar focus 1
Past simple – positive and negative

1 Complete the past forms of the verbs below. Some of the verbs are regular and some are irregular.

1	appear	appear_e d_	11	find	f_ _nd	21	make	ma_ _
2	begin	beg_n	12	forget	forg_ _	22	meet	m_ _
3	buy	bou_ _t	13	get	g_t	23	play	play_ _
4	come	c_me	14	go	we_ _	24	read	r_ _d
5	cost	c_st	15	happen	happen_ _	25	sing	s_ng
6	die	di_ _	16	invent	invent_ _	26	stay	stay_ _
7	drive	dr_ve	17	know	kn_w	27	take	t_ _k
8	eat	_t_	18	live	liv_ _	28	think	tho_ _ _t
9	fall	fe_ _	19	look	look_ _	29	work	work_ _
10	feel	fe_ _	20	lose	lo_ _	30	write	wr_t_

2a Complete the text with the Past simple form of the verbs in brackets.

The first TV soap opera

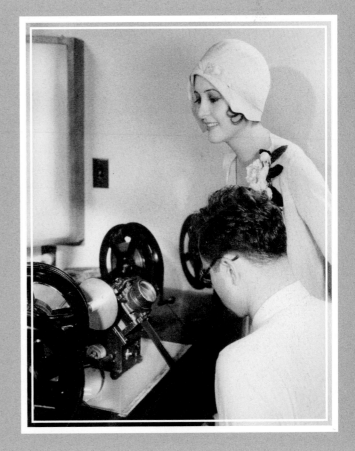

The first TV soap opera [1] *appeared* (appear) on American television just after the Second World War. Its name [2] _____ (be) *Faraway Hill* and it [3] _____ (begin) on 2nd October 1946.

A famous Broadway actress, Flora Campbell, [4] _____ (play) Karen St. John, a rich New York woman who [5] _____ (go) to live with her relatives in the country after her husband [6] _____ (die). She soon [7] _____ (meet) a handsome young farmer and, of course, the two immediately [8] _____ (fall) in love. Unfortunately, the farmer [9] _____ (be) already engaged to Karen's cousin, who [10] _____ (know) nothing about the relationship. When she [11] _____ (find out), things [12] _____ (get) very, very difficult for Karen.

The producers of *Faraway Hill* [13] _____ (have) very little money - each programme [14] _____ (cost) only 300 dollars - so they [15] _____ (make) them as quickly as possible. Because there [16] _____ (be) no time for the actors to learn their words each week, assistants [17] _____ (write) them on blackboards. Because of this, they often [18] _____ (look) into the distance with a strange, romantic expression on their faces ... as they [19] _____ (read) their words from the boards on the other side of the studio!

b 🎧 2.1 Now listen and check.

c Correct the sentences about *Faraway Hill*.

1 The first TV soap opera appeared before the Second World War.

It didn't appear before the Second World War.
It appeared after the Second World War.

2 Its name was *Faraway Land*.

_____
_____
_____

3 It began in October 1936.

_____
_____
_____

4 It was about a rich farmer who moved to New York.

_____
_____
_____

5 The woman went to live with her friends.

_____
_____
_____

6 She fell in love with her cousin.

_____
_____
_____

7 The farmer was married to her cousin.

_____
_____
_____

8 The producers of the programme had a lot of money.

_____
_____
_____

9 Each programme cost 500 dollars.

_____
_____
_____

10 The assistants wrote the actors' words on pieces of paper.

_____
_____
_____

3 Make sentences in the Past simple using the prompts.

1 I / write down / her phone number (her name)

I wrote down her phone number, but I didn't write down her name.

2 we / visit / the museum (the castle)

_____
_____

3 I / see / Samantha (Kevin)

_____
_____

4 they / invite / Nick to their party (Ella)

_____
_____

5 I / like / the film (the music)

_____
_____

6 he / buy / a present for Kate (one for me)

_____
_____

7 she / clean / her room (the living room)

_____
_____

8 I / know / the boy (his sister)

_____
_____

Pronunciation
-ed endings

4a Look at the Past simple verbs ending in /d/, /t/ and /ɪd/. One verb in each group is different. <u>Underline</u> the different one.

1 worked	laughed	stopped	<u>wanted</u>
2 called	asked	lived	closed
3 ended	started	opened	lasted
4 walked	arrived	travelled	appeared
5 watched	looked	invented	laughed

b 🎧 2.2 Listen and check.

Vocabulary

Times phrases: *at, on, in, ago*

5 Answer at least six of the questions below about yourself. Use *ago* in your answers.

1 When did you first start learning English?
I first started learning English three years ago.

2 When did you first learn to write?
_____

3 When did you first use a computer?
_____

4 When did you first send an email?
_____

5 When did you first go abroad?
_____

6 When did you last watch or listen to the news?
_____

7 When did you last make a phone call?
_____

8 When did you last wash your hands?
_____

9 When did you last watch a film?
_____

10 When did you last write a letter to a friend?
_____

6 Complete the sentences with *at, on, in* or – .

1 My grandmother was born ___*in*___ 1939.
2 I got up today _____ 8.30.
3 I met Kerry in the street _____ last week – she looked very well.
4 They got married _____ a year ago.
5 I had a doctor's appointment _____ Friday morning.
6 January was very cold _____ this year.
7 I was born _____ 30th April.
8 Bob moved to Budapest _____ the 1970s.

Grammar focus 2

Past simple – questions

7 Put the words in the correct order to make questions.

1 you / do / What / did / yesterday?
What did you do yesterday?

2 did / go / you / Where?
_____

3 say / What / did / she?
_____

4 good / party / the / Was?
_____

5 your / you / husband / meet / did / How?
_____

6 the / film / enjoy / they / Did?
_____

7 tickets / did / cost / How / the / much?
_____

8 late / Why / you / were?
_____

9 the / time / What / game / finish / did?
_____

10 lunch / with / did / have / you / Who?
_____

8a Choose the correct answers.

1 What *was* / *did* the film *The Iron Lady* about?
2 Who *was* / *did* Margaret Thatcher?
3 Why did people *called* / *call* her 'the iron lady'?
4 Who *did act* / *acted* as Margaret Thatcher in the film?
5 How old was she when she *made* / *did make* the film?
6 Did Mrs Thatcher *like* / *liked* the film?
7 Who *directed* / *did direct* the film?
8 *Did* / *Was* the film successful?

b Match the answers with the questions in exercise a.

a She was 62. ☐
b I don't know if she has seen it. ☐
c The director was Phyllida Lloyd. ☐
d Yes, it was, and it won two Oscars. ☐
e Because she was a very strong woman. ☐
f The American actress Meryl Streep did. ☐
g It tells the story of the life of Margaret Thatcher. ☐ 1
h She was the Prime Minister of Britain from 1979 to 1990. ☐

9a Make questions in the Past simple using the prompts.

1 what time / you / get up / this morning?
   What time did you get up this morning?
2 what time / you / go / to bed / last night?
   _____
3 you / be / at home / on Sunday morning?
   _____
4 when / you / have / your first birthday party?
   _____
5 how old / you / be / in 2009?
   _____
6 you / go out / last night?
   _____
7 when / you / last / see / your best friend?
   _____
8 what / you / do / last weekend?
   _____
9 what / you / have / for lunch / yesterday?
   _____
10 your friend / call / you / yesterday?
   _____

b Answer the questions in exercise a.

1 _____
2 _____
3 _____
4 _____
5 _____
6 _____
7 _____
8 _____
9 _____
10 _____

Vocabulary
Words to describe feelings

10 Choose the correct answers.

1 When Amanda didn't come home from her night out, her parents felt very **bored /** **worried**.

2 The night before her birthday, Anna was so **stressed / excited** she couldn't sleep.

3 After a terrible day at work, I got home, listened to some music and had a bath. Then I felt more **relaxed / excited**.

4 I wanted a new DVD player for my birthday, but all I got was a stupid computer game! I was really **embarrassed / disappointed**.

5 She was late, tired and hungry. That's why she was **worried / in a bad mood**.

6 It was a beautiful sunny day and as I walked across the park, I was **in a good mood / in a bad mood**.

7 The film was nearly three hours long. A lot of people got **disappointed / bored** and left before the end.

8 I was **surprised / scared** to see David in London. I thought he was in Paris!

9 Frank woke up and heard a noise downstairs. He was very **scared / angry** and he couldn't move.

10 My new haircut looked horrible! I was too **embarrassed / surprised** to go out.

11 I'm sorry. I lost the CD you lent me. Please don't be **relaxed / angry**.

12 People often feel a little **in a bad mood / stressed** before an important exam.

Language live
Travel questions

11a Read the questions. One word is missing from each question. Add the word in the correct place.

1 Have you your passport?
   Have you got your passport?

2 Did you have nice time?
   _____

3 How your flight?
   _____

4 Time's your taxi?
   _____

5 What do you arrive?
   _____

6 Where you staying?
   _____

7 Are you here business?
   _____

8 Is your first time here?
   _____

b Do you ask the questions in exercise a before, during or after someone's journey? Write *b* (before), *d* (during) or *a* (after).

1 *b*   4 ___   7 ___
2 ___   5 ___   8 ___
3 ___   6 ___

Writing
A narrative

12a Complete the text with the words in the box.

because	and	so	then	but

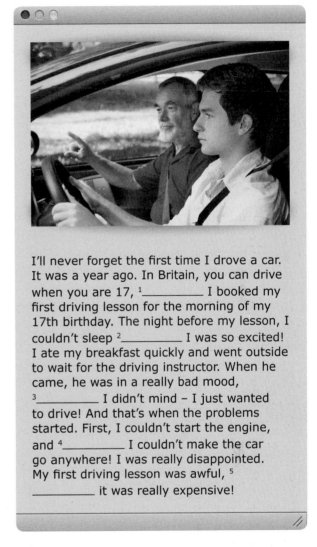

I'll never forget the first time I drove a car. It was a year ago. In Britain, you can drive when you are 17, ¹_____ I booked my first driving lesson for the morning of my 17th birthday. The night before my lesson, I couldn't sleep ²_____ I was so excited! I ate my breakfast quickly and went outside to wait for the driving instructor. When he came, he was in a really bad mood, ³_____ I didn't mind – I just wanted to drive! And that's when the problems started. First, I couldn't start the engine, and ⁴_____ I couldn't make the car go anywhere! I was really disappointed. My first driving lesson was awful, ⁵ _____ it was really expensive!

b Now write a paragraph about doing something difficult for the first time. Use the words and phrases in the box.

and   so   but   because   then
Finally, ...   I'll never forget ...
It was about ... years ago.   I was very ... because ...
I was about ... years old at the time.

03 WORK AND REST

Vocabulary
Daily routines

1a Complete the phrases with the words in the box.

> asleep nap energetic work to bed up (x2) home
> to eat a shower

   1 wake ____*up*____
   2 fall _____
   3 have a _____
   4 have _____
   5 have something _____
   6 feel _____
   7 get _____
   8 relax at _____
   9 go _____
  10 finish _____

b Dave works at night printing newspapers. Complete the text about his routine with phrases from exercise a.

> I started a new job two months ago; I work nights. I get to work at 8 in the evening and I ¹_____ at 5:30 in the morning. When I get home, I'm not tired though, because it's usually getting light and I don't want to sleep. In fact, I ²_____ and usually go for a run. When I come back, I ³_____ and change my clothes. Then I ⁴_____ , but I'm not sure if it's breakfast or supper! After my meal I normally feel quite tired, so I ⁵_____ at about 9. I always read the newspaper for an hour or so. In fact, sometimes I ⁶_____ while I'm reading! I don't have an alarm clock and I always ⁷_____ between 4 and 5 in the afternoon and usually read a bit more. I ⁸_____ at about 6, then start getting ready for work. My job's great – we have long breaks, so if I'm tired, I can usually ⁹_____ for 20 minutes or so, and then I feel much better. And at weekends I don't go anywhere – I just ¹⁰_____ in front of the TV.

Grammar focus 1
should, shouldn't

2 You are having dinner with people you don't know well. Which of the things below should you do and which shouldn't you do in your culture?

  1 You _*shouldn't*_ speak with your mouth full.
  2 You _____ wait for the others before you start eating.
  3 You _____ eat with your fingers.
  4 You _____ eat with your elbows on the table.
  5 You _____ make a noise when you drink something.
  6 You _____ put the knife in your mouth.
  7 You _____ use a spoon for soup.
  8 You _____ put your knife and fork on the plate when you finish.

3 Match the sentence halves.

  1 If you want to have healthy teeth, you   ☑ f
  2 I'm feeling tired – I think I   ☐
  3 I want to be a nurse – what qualifications   ☐
  4 I'm hungry – shouldn't we   ☐
  5 You shouldn't drink   ☐
  6 Which bus should   ☐
  7 There's a problem with the bathroom – I think we should   ☐

  a we get?
  b should I get?
  c phone a plumber.
  d should go to bed.
  e have something to eat?
  f should go to the dentist twice a year.
  g coffee at night – you won't fall asleep!

Listen and read
My favourite days of the week

4a 🎧 3.1 Read and listen to the article.

My favourite days of the week
We asked three local people about their favourite day of the week. Here's what they said:

Amy, 28

Well, most people say their favourite day is Saturday or Sunday, when they have a break from work. Of course I love my weekends, but I think my favourite day of the week is actually Friday. I'm an accountant in an office and there's always a great atmosphere because it's the end of the week and people are excited about the weekend. Everyone's talking about their plans, that sort of thing. And we even look different – we all wear smart clothes from Monday to Thursday, but on Fridays it's OK to wear anything we want. Most people just come in jeans and T-shirts. And we all go out together at the end of the day. Some of my colleagues are just so funny!

Darek, 19

I'm a waiter, so my working hours are different to most people's. Basically, if most people are relaxing, I'm working! So in the restaurant, Fridays and weekends are a really busy time – we have a lot of parties, so we work long hours. It's fun because people are enjoying themselves. Sundays are a bit quieter. And then on Mondays the restaurant is closed and that's the best part of my week. I usually get up late, relax at home and maybe have a nap in the afternoon if I'm tired. I don't do much – just watch films – but sometimes that's exactly what I need. Perhaps it's not very healthy – I want to start playing football or something. Maybe I will, on Thursday afternoons.

Pietro, 38

Like everyone, I enjoy my weekends, but they're never very relaxing. There's always so much to do: tidying the house, getting meals ready, that sort of thing, because we often invite relatives round for lunch on Sundays. But the day I enjoy the most is Tuesday. I work different times every day and that's the day I finish early. I pick my kids up from school and take them swimming and we always have such a great time together. And when I'm back at work on Wednesday morning, I always feel better.

b Match the people (1–3) with their favourite day.

1 Amy ☐ 2 Darek ☐ 3 Pietro ☐

a Monday	**e** Friday
b Tuesday	**f** Saturday
c Wednesday	**g** Sunday
d Thursday	

c Who:

1 can leave work early one day a week? _____
2 has to go to work at weekends? _____
3 thinks he/she should do some sport? _____
4 goes out with his/her colleagues once a week? _____
5 has to do lots of things at home at weekends? _____
6 doesn't have to wear smart clothes at work every day? _____

Grammar focus 2
can, can't, have to, don't have to

5a Rewrite the sentences replacing the phrase in bold with *can* or *can't* and any other necessary words.

1 **Is it possible** to borrow your dictionary?
   Can I borrow your dictionary?

2 My sister **is able to** speak three languages perfectly.

3 **It's impossible for me to** do this exercise!

4 Now **it is possible for you to** buy cheap plane tickets on the internet.

5 **It's impossible for Renate to** come to the party.

6 **Are you able to** read French? I don't understand this.

7 **We're not able to** answer the phone at the moment.

8 **Is it possible for us to** sit by the window?

9 Only students **have permission to** use the library.

10 **You don't have permmission to** come in here.

b 🎧 3.2 Listen and check. Practise saying the sentences.

6a Jodie is still at school. Her older brother, Ed, left school last month. Complete the conversation with *have to/don't have to* and the verbs in the box.

~~get up~~ answer be do find try wear (x2) worry (x2) write

Jodie: You're so lucky! You ¹*don't have to get up* early every day and go to school.

Ed: Yes, I know, but now I ²_____ a job.

Jodie: That's not so bad. At least you ³_____ homework every night.

Ed: True, but I ⁴_____ application letters and make lots of phone calls. It's boring!

Jodie: Not as boring as school! And you ⁵_____ a horrible uniform!

Ed: Well, no, but I ⁶_____ smart clothes when I go to a job interview.

Jodie: Hmm ... But you ⁷_____ the teacher's questions all day.

Ed: What about the questions at the interview? I ⁸_____ to answer those.

Jodie: OK, but you ⁹_____ about exams.

Ed: And you ¹⁰_____ about earning money.

Jodie: Well, I ¹¹_____ good all week so Mum and Dad give me my pocket money!

b 🎧 3.3 Listen and check.

7 Ben is going to take his driving test soon. Complete the conversation with the correct form of *have to* or *can*.

Ben: Is it true that there are two driving tests?

Instructor: That's right: you [1]*have to* take a written test and a practical test – that's where you're on the road with the examiner.

Ben: [2]_____ I take the practical test first, please?

Instructor: No, I'm sorry. You [3]_____ take that test until you've passed the written one.

Ben: Hmm ... Is the written test very difficult?

Instructor: No, not really. There are 50 questions, but the good news is you [4]_____ answer all of them correctly. You [5]_____ get 45 correct answers, so you [6]_____ make a few mistakes and still pass.

Ben: [7]_____ you give me some advice about how to prepare for the written exam?

Instructor: Learn all the rules of the road! But there are thousands, so you [8]_____ remember everything at once – you [9]_____ study a little bit every day.

Ben: OK. How about the practical exam?

Instructor: Well, on the day, the examiner [10]_____ see your driving licence. Then he asks you to read a number plate to check you [11]_____ see OK.

Ben: That sounds easy. [12]_____ I take my test straight away?

Instructor: Impossible! You [13]_____ learn to park first – you won't pass if you [14]_____ park your car!

Pronunciation
can, have to

8a 🎧 **3.4** Listen to the sentences. What do you hear: *can* or *can't*?

1 can	☐	can't	☐
2 can	☐	can't	☐
3 can	☐	can't	☐
4 can	☐	can't	☐
5 can	☐	can't	☐

b 🎧 **3.5** Listen to the sentences. What do you hear: a or b?

1 You **can** finish work early today.
   a /kæn/   **ⓑ** /kən/

2 I **can**? Excellent, thank you!
   a / kæn /   **b** /kən/

3 I have **to** eat something. I'm so hungry.
   a /tuː/   **b** /tə/

4 Well, then you have **to** cook something!
   a /tuː/   **b** /tə/

5 **Can** you speak French?
   a / kæn /   **b** / kən /

6 Yes, of course I **can**. I'm a translator.
   a´/ kæn /   **b** /kən/

7 Come on, you have **to** do your homework now.
   a /tuː/   **b** /tə/

8 Oh, Dad, do I have **to**?
   a /tuː/   **b** /tə/

9 Excuse me, where **can** I get something to eat?
   a / kæn /   **b** /kən/

10 You **can** try that café over there. It's very good.
   a / kæn /   **b** /kən/

Vocabulary
Jobs

9 Read the texts and write the jobs in the grid.

1
Janina, 25, Poland

I work in a restaurant. We serve Italian food and I work in the kitchen making it. I make a lot of pizzas and some pasta dishes. It's a great job with really nice people. When I finish in the evening, I can eat some of the food I have prepared.

2
Bob, 63, England

The worst thing about my job is that people usually only call me when they have a problem in their kitchen or bathroom. The other night, someone called me at 10 p.m. to tell me that their washing machine wasn't working. Water was coming out of it. But the best thing about my job is finishing a new bathroom or kitchen and seeing that my customers are pleased.

3
Howard, 42, Jamaica

I've always done this job. Before, I had a taxi, but now I drive a bus. It's a nice job because you meet lots of people. But sometimes I have to work evenings and weekends and then I don't spend time with my family.

4
Tomoko, 29, Japan

A lot of people think this job is boring. But I love it! I've always liked maths, so working with numbers all day is no problem for me. Lots of working people don't have time to deal with their money and taxes. So that's how I can help.

5
Marisa, 20, Philippines

I've looked after children all my life. When I was a child, I helped my parents with my five younger brothers and sisters. And now, looking after other people's children is my job. I work for a family with two children. The parents work full-time, so I take the older child to school and then spend the rest of the day with the younger one. She's two and she's learning to speak. I think I've got the best job in the world!

6
Marwan, 58, Egypt

People think that I work in court every day. In fact, I am in my office most days. I only go to court once or twice a week. But this is when I have to make important decisions. So I always need to listen very carefully to people.

7
Maria, 33, Argentina

I studied languages at university. My first language is Spanish and I also know Portuguese and Chinese. There is a lot of business between my country and Brazil. But a lot of people in Argentina don't understand Portuguese. So my job is to read documents in Portuguese and then write the same thing in Spanish.

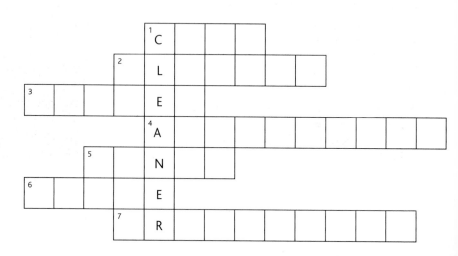

04 SPECIAL DAYS

Pronunciation
Days and dates

1a 🎧 **4.1 Listen to the months and put the words in groups according to the stress.**

Ooo	O	Oo	oO	oOo
January				*September*

b 🎧 **4.2 Listen to the pronunciation of *th* in these dates. Do you hear /θ/ or /ð/ ?**

1 the _ð_ sixteen**th** _θ_ of November
2 May **the** ____ second
3 December **the** ____ fif**th** ____
4 **the** ____ **th**irty-first ____ of May
5 **the** ____ **th**irteen**th** ____ , ____ of August
6 June **the** ____ **th**ird ____

Vocabulary
Verb phrases for special days

2a **Choose the correct answers.**

1 I don't usually **write** / ⬭**send** cards by post – I do it via the internet.
2 Emma didn't feel like cooking last night, so we ate **up** / **out**.
3 You look really tired. I think you should have a day **off** / **of** work.
4 I'm going to **exchange** / **prepare** a special meal for him tomorrow – it's his birthday.
5 He **exchanged** / **invited** Mr Edwards to his house for lunch.
6 On the last day of school, the students **exchanged** / **invited** presents.
7 I'm **making** / **doing** a chocolate cake for Stephen – his favourite!
8 You don't have to dress **up** / **out** – you can come as you are.
9 She went to Brighton last month to visit her **presents** / **relatives**.
10 Dad always **prepares** / **buys** flowers for Mum on her birthday.

b **Complete the sentences with the correct form of the words in the box.**

have ~~dress~~ buy visit send eat make
invite prepare exchange

1 At the Carnival, many people __*dress*__ up in colourful clothes.
2 It was Grandma's birthday yesterday. Did you remember to _____ her a birthday card?
3 At the weekend, I often _____ relatives. I went to see my aunt last Sunday.
4 When I passed all my exams, my mum _____ a special meal for me.
5 At the end of the course, our teacher _____ everyone in the class to her house for dinner.
6 Last December, the schools closed because there was lots of snow one day. So lots of children _____ a day off school.
7 It's Valentine's Day tomorrow, so don't forget to _____ some flowers for your wife!
8 Charlie's mum is going to _____ a special cake for his birthday.
9 My family and I often _____ out as there are lots of cheap restaurants near our home.
10 Most people in Britain spend Christmas Day with their families and after lunch, they often _____ presents.

Grammar focus 1
Present simple and Present continuous

3 Complete the conversations with the Present continuous form of the verbs brackets.

1 **A:** _Are you enjoying_ (you / enjoy) yourselves?
   B: Oh, yes! We ____'re having____ (have) a fantastic time, thank you!

2 **A:** I'm sorry, _____ (I / drive) too fast for you?
   B: Yes, _____ . Could you slow down?

3 **A:** What _____ (you / do)?
   B: There's a film on TV, but I _____ (not watch) it, really.

4 **A:** What's the problem?
   B: I _____ (look for) my keys. _____ (you / sit) on them?
   A: Oh, yes, here they are. Sorry!

5 It's Sunday, so Jo _____ (not work) today. She _____ (spend) some time at home for a change.

6 **A:** Where _____ (you / go)?
   B: Shopping. Do you want to come?
   A: I can't. My parents _____ (wait) for me.

7 **A:** _____ (you / talk) to me?
   B: Yes, _____ . And you _____ (not listen)!

8 **A:** Why _____ (that man / look) at us?
   B: He _____ (not look) at us. His wife _____ (sit) right behind us.

4 Choose the correct answers.

1 **A:** So, what other languages **are you speaking** / ⟨**do you speak**⟩?
   B: English, French and Italian.

2 **A:** Ow!
   B: What's the matter? What **do you do** / **are you doing**?

3 **A:** What's that song **you listen** / **you're listening** to?
   B: It's called *Angels*. Good, isn't it?

4 **A:** What **are you writing** / **do you write**?
   B: It's a story for the school magazine.

5 **A:** **Do you eat** / **Are you eating** meat?
   B: No, I stopped eating meat two years ago.

6 **A:** Why **are you laughing** / **do you laugh**?
   B: It's your face. You look so funny!

7 **A:** **Does your brother play** / **Is your brother playing** any sport?
   B: Yes. Football in the winter, tennis in the summer and swimming all year.

8 **A:** Paul? **Are you listening** / **Do you listen** to me?
   B: Hmm? What? Sorry?

5 Tick (✓) the correct sentences. Correct the sentences that are wrong.

1 Do you like coffee? ✓
   _____

2 Are you having any brothers or sisters? ☐
   Do you have any brothers or sisters?

3 I'm not believing you! ☐
   _____

4 Do you want to come with us tonight? ☐
   _____

5 I'm not understanding this exercise. ☐
   _____

6 I'm hating cold weather. ☐
   _____

7 I don't know her name. ☐
   _____

6 Complete the sentences with the Present simple or Present continuous form of the verbs in brackets.

1 Hurry up! They _are waiting_ (wait) for us!

2 I _____ (not want) to go to the cinema. Let's watch a DVD.

3 My brother _____ (love) jazz.

4 Ella is in her room. She _____ (study) for her English test.

5 Yes, I _____ (understand) now, thank you.

6 He's at home. He _____ (not work) today.

7 Let's go. We _____ (not have) much time.

8 'What _____ (you / read)?' 'An article about holidays in Switzerland.'

Vocabulary
Descriptive adjectives

7a Look at the phrases. Cross out one adjective in each group which cannot go with the noun.

1. boiling
   ~~friendly~~   weather
   freezing

2. exciting
   tasty   atmosphere
   peaceful

3. noisy
   tasty   food
   spicy

4. noisy
   delicious   party
   friendly

5. peaceful
   boiling   soup
   spicy

6. noisy
   peaceful   town
   delicious

b Match the sentence halves.

1. The house was freezing, ☐
2. It was a really friendly ☐
3. This cake is delicious! How ☐
4. We stayed in a really peaceful ☐
5. My neighbours often play noisy ☐

a. did you make it?
b. so I turned the heating on.
c. party and I met some nice people.
d. music at night – it's really annoying!
e. hotel in the mountains and just relaxed.

c Choose the correct answers.

1. It's *freezing* / *boiling* outside! Put your coat on.
2. I love that restaurant – it's got good food and a very *friendly* / *delicious* atmosphere.
3. Life here isn't very *tasty* / *exciting* – there's nothing to do!
4. The meat was OK, but I didn't like the sauce – it was too *spicy* / *noisy* for me.
5. It was a great party. The music was brilliant and the food was *boiling* / *delicious*.
6. Oh dear, it's *spicy* / *boiling* in here! Open a window!
7. The streets were *noisy* / *peaceful* and full of traffic.
8. It's always so *tasty* / *peaceful* out here in the country.

Grammar focus 2
Present continuous for future arrangements

8 Complete the sentences with the Present continuous form of the verbs in brackets.

1. We *are taking* (take) the kids to the theatre on Saturday.
2. I have to study for my English exam, so I _____ (not go) to Nick's party.
3. _____ (you / come) with us tonight?
4. My grandparents _____ (fly) to London tomorrow.
5. He _____ (drive) Lisa and Ben to the airport at 6 p.m.
6. What _____ (you / do) tomorrow?
7. They're in Paris. They _____ (come back) on Friday.
8. Where _____ (you / go) on holiday next year? Have you decided yet?
9. No, she _____ (not stay) with us. She wants to stay in a hotel.
10. _____ (your dad / work) next Sunday?

9a Look at the family calendar for next week. Write sentences about the four family members, like this:

Steve isn't working on Monday. He's playing squash
with Andy at 10:30
_____
_____
_____
_____
_____
_____

Judy _____
_____
_____
_____
_____

Steve and Judy _____
_____
_____
_____

Oliver _____
_____
_____
_____

Florence _____
_____

Oliver and Florence _____
_____

The whole family _____
_____

	STEVE	JUDY	OLIVER	FLORENCE
Mon 7	*No work! Squash with Andy. 10:30*	*work*		*swimming*
Tues 8	*to Manchester for the day. Train at 6:45.*		*football at 4 o'clock*	
Wed 9		*work*	*to Tom's house after school*	
Thurs 10	*cinema with Jan and Chris (Steve's mum to babysit)*			
Fri 11		*meet Alison for lunch – 1 o'clock*	*meeting cousins in the park at 2:30*	
Sat 12				
Sun 13	*Lunch with grandparents at 12 o'clock*			

b 🎧 4.3 Practise saying the sentences.

10a Put the words in the correct order to make questions.

1 going / you / Where / your / are / this / holidays / year / for?
   Where are you going for your holidays this year?
2 you / week / a / having / Are / this / off / day?
   _____
3 next / you / doing / What / weekend / are?
   _____
4 future / to / relatives / visit / coming / Are / near / your / in / the?
   _____
5 are / lesson / English / When / next / having / you / your?
   _____
6 meeting / today / you / friends / later / Are / your?
   _____
7 dinner / in / evening / Who's / your / cooking / house / this?
   _____
8 anyone / the / month / Is / this / dentist / your / going / family / in / to?
   _____

b Answer the questions in exercise a.

1 _____
2 _____
3 _____
4 _____
5 _____
6 _____
7 _____
8 _____

Language live
Phrases for special days

11a Complete the conversations with the phrases in the box.

....
Safe journey!   Happy New Year   Thanks for inviting me.
I hope you'll be very happy   Many happy returns
....

1 **A:** Congratulations on your wedding!
  _____ together.
  B: Thanks, and I'm sure we will!

2 **A:** _____ to you on your birthday!
  B: Thanks. I can't believe I'm 40 already!

3 **A:** I hope you enjoyed the party.
  B: Yes, it was great. _____ You must come
  to my home some time.

4 **A:** _____ to you. I hope it's going to be a
  good one.
  B: Thanks, and to you, too.

5 **A:** Thanks for coming. _____
  B: Don't worry. I always drive carefully.

b 🎧 4.4 Listen and check.

Writing
An invitation

12a Read the invitation to Silvia's wedding. Then look
at the replies from two of Silvia's friends, Igor and
Jennifer. Put the sections in the right order.

Silvia & Dominic

would like to invite you to their wedding

on Saturday 19th June
3:30 p.m

Barnford Town Hall
34 High Street
Barnford

And then a reception at
Derry's Restaurant
5 Beechen Road
Barnford

RSVP silvia@uk4mail.com

New Message

Dear Silvia,

Thanks very much for inviting me, but,
unfortunately,

1 ___f___
2 _____
3 _____
4 _____
5 _____
6 _____

an email and let me know?

All the best,
Igor

New Message

Hi Silvia,

What great news! Congratulations!
I hope you'll

7 ___h___
8 _____
9 _____
10 _____
11 _____
12 _____
See you then.

Love,
Jennifer

a   come. Life here is
b   make it. Can you send me
c   to see you. We're having a
d   me, and yes, please, I'd love to
e   and Dominic come? I hope you can
f   I can't come because my family and I are
g   going on holiday that week. But we'd love
h   be very happy together. Thanks for inviting
i   very busy and I'm really, really tired! My big
j   in touch again soon. I can't wait until 19th July!
k   dinner party on Saturday 24th July. Why don't you
l   news is that I've moved to a new house. Anyway,
    I'll be

b **Now write your own reply to Silvia.**

Listen and read

Stars 4 U

1 🎧 **5.1 Read and listen to the text and choose the correct answers.**

1 The text is
  A an advert.
  B an article.
  C a short story.

2 Who are John, Norman and Eliza?
  A famous people
  B people who look like famous people
  C customers of Stars 4 U

3 What do you do if you want John Anster to come to your party?
  A contact him
  B contact Stars 4 U
  C ask him if you see him in the street

4 Why does the text include a list of famous people?
  A to say which look-alikes are available
  B to show which famous people have used Stars 4 U
  C to find more look-alikes

5 What did Stars 4 U do for Emma Montford?
  A They invited her to a party.
  B They sent her two guests for her party.
  C They gave her a job as a look-alike.

STARS 4 U

At Stars 4 U, we find our customers someone who looks like a famous person.

Do you want Barack Obama to come to your office party? Well, that might be difficult – he's probably too busy! But with Stars 4 U, it's no problem. We can let you have our Barack Obama look-alike, John Anster. John looks exactly like Obama. When John walks down the street, people can't believe it – they think it's Obama! People always look so surprised when they see him. 'Excuse me, is it really you?' they often ask.

But John doesn't just look the same as Obama. He sounds very similar to Obama, too! He works as a professional Barack Obama look-alike. And John can come to your party or conference at your college, home or workplace. Just contact us at info@stars4u.com. Tell us who you want, where and when, and we'll send you our price.

We also have look-alikes for the following stars:

Music:	Beyoncé, Gotye, Adele, Michael Jackson	**Sport:**	Maria Sharapova, Rafael Nadal, David Beckham
Film:	Sean Connery, Sharukh Khan, Johnny Depp	**VIPs:**	Prince William and Catherine, Duchess of Cambridge

But don't just believe us! We've had hundreds of satisfied customers. You can read what they said about Stars 4 U on our website, www.stars4u.com. Here's what one of them said:

'Thank you, Stars 4 U! When I had my 21st birthday party, I wanted to do something different, so I contacted Stars 4 U. They sent me Prince William and Catherine, Duchess of Cambridge look-alikes, Norman and Eliza. It was amazing and worth the money. My friends couldn't believe the British Royal family were at my party! Thank you, Stars 4 U – it was brilliant!'

Emma Montford, New York, USA

Vocabulary
Physical appearance

2 Cross out the word that does not belong in each group.

1	dyed	wavy	slim	straight	curly
2	moustache	slim	tall	bald	clean-shaven
3	glasses	tattoo	hair	piercings	lipstick
4	pale	dark	fair	tall	white

3 Use the clues to complete the grid below.

1 If hair isn't straight or curly, but has gentle curves, it is _____ .

2 Hair between a man's mouth and nose.

3 If someone has no hair on their head, they are _____ .

4 A picture that is put onto someone's skin using a needle.

5 Holes on your body for putting jewellery in.

6 What you wear in front of your eyes to help you see.

7 If hair isn't wavy or curly, it is _____ .

8 _____ skin is very light in colour.

9 _____ hair is pale or yellow.

10 This word can describe hair or skin that is light in colour.

11 Women use _____ to paint their lips.

12 If your hair is _____ , you have changed its colour.

The vertical word spells: W H A T I S H E L I K E ?

Grammar focus 1
Comparative and superlative adjectives

4a Read the profiles of two boxers, Paul Chang and Mike 'The Monster' Morton. Write questions and answers using the adjectives in brackets.

	Paul Chang	Mike 'The Monster' Morton
Age	19	36
Height	1.85 m	1.78 m
Speed	very fast	slow
Experience	not very experienced	very experienced
Weight	80 kg	95 kg
Aggression factor	80%	90%
Power rating	7/10	9/10
Popularity	☺ ☺ ☺	☺

Who is ...

1 (old) _older?_

Mike is older than Paul.

2 (young) _____

_____

3 (tall) _____

_____

4 (fast) _____

_____

5 (experienced) _____

_____

6 (slow) _____

_____

7 (heavy) _____

_____

8 (aggressive) _____

_____

9 (powerful) _____

_____

10 (popular) _____

_____

b 🎧 5.2 **Practise saying the sentences.**

5 **Complete the sentences with the superlative form of the adjectives in brackets.**

1 The ___ _tallest_ ___ (tall) US President was Abraham Lincoln, who was 1.93m, and the ___ _oldest_ ___ (old) was Ronald Reagan, who was 69 when he became President in 1981.

2 The _____ (fast) winner of a London Marathon was the Kenyan runner Emmanuel Mutai – ten minutes better than the _____ (quick) woman, Paula Radcliffe from the UK.

3 Sultan Hassanal Bolkiah, Sultan of the Arab state of Brunei, is the world's _____ (rich) monarch. Many people think that Queen Elizabeth of the United Kingdom is the _____ (wealthy) female ruler.

4 Elvis Presley, who died in 1977, was probably the _____ (popular) singer of all time. He always said that the _____ (important) person in his life was his mother.

5 Queen Jane had the _____ (short) time on the throne of any English Queen: just five days! King Louis XIV of France was King for the _____ (long) time: 72 years!

6 Guinness World Records described Paul McCartney as _____ (successful) songwriter of all time. McCartney was a member of The Beatles, one of _____ (great) rock bands in the history of music.

7 Tom Cruise, one of Hollywood's _____ (famous) actors, is also one of the world's _____ (high) paid actors: between May 2011 and May 2012, he earned 75 million dollars!

6 🎧 **5.3 Here are some famous sayings which contain a comparative or superlative adjective. Listen and underline the comparative and superlative forms.**

> 1 Democracy is <u>the worst</u> form of government … apart from all the others.
>
> *Winston Churchill*

> 2 The reason I wanted to be an actress was to play people much more interesting than I am and to say things much more intelligent than anything I could think of myself.

Actress Prunella Scales

> 3 All animals are equal, but some are more equal than others.
>
> *George Orwell in* Animal Farm

> 4 Good, better, the best
> Never let it rest
> Until good is better
> And better is the best

Unknown teacher

> 5 Being funny is much more difficult than being clever.
>
> *Editor of a comedy magazine*

7 **Complete the sentences with *as*, *than*, *from*, *like*, *in* or *to*.**

1 Helen is the tallest person __*in*__ our class.
2 She has the same taste in clothes _____ me.
3 Anna is older _____ she looks.
4 Marie's dress is very similar __*to*__ mine.
5 Do you look _____ your parents?
6 Who's the youngest person _____ your family?
7 Our lives today are very different _____ the way our grandparents lived.
8 Are these glasses the same _____ yours?

Pronunciation
Weak forms in sentences

8a 🎧 **5.4 Listen to Adam talking to his friend. What is the problem?**

A He doesn't like his haircut.
B He is annoyed with his father.
C He has argued with his friend Boris.

b **Now listen again. Are the underlined words stressed or unstressed?**

Jane: Adam? Hi, it's Jane here.
Adam: Oh, hi, Jane. Oh, you know what, I've just had a haircut.
Jane: Cool! What's it like?
Adam: Well, shorter <u>than</u> before.
Jane: Yeah, of course!
Adam: I wanted a haircut the same <u>as</u> my friend Boris's – you know.
Jane: Right.
Adam: Well, it isn't. In fact, it's probably the worst haircut <u>in</u> the world!
Jane: Why?
Adam: Well, the thing is, with this new haircut, I look very similar <u>to</u> my dad.
Jane: Oh, come on, your dad's great!
Adam: Yeah, I know, but I don't want to look <u>like</u> him!

Grammar focus 2

Questions with *How*, *What* and *What ... like?*

9a Write the questions for the answers about Donna.

1 *How old is she?*
She's in her twenties.

2 _____
She's slim and athletic-looking.

3 _____
About 1.75 m.

4 _____
She's very friendly.

5 _____
No, it isn't very long.

6 _____
They're dark brown.

b 🎧 5.5 Listen and check. Then listen and practise saying the questions.

10a Complete the conversation between Mrs Ogden (MO) and a police officer (PO). Write questions with *How, What* or *What ... like?* and the words in brackets.

PO: So, tell me about the man who stole your neighbour's car. ¹*What did he look like?* (look like)

MO: He was tall and slim. And he was very handsome!

PO: ² _____ (tall)

MO: Well, he was about as tall as you.

PO: OK. ³ _____ (hair)

MO: Long, black and wavy. But he was clean-shaven. I don't like men with beards!

PO: Right, so with long wavy hair and no beard.
⁴ _____ (colour / eyes)

MO: Oh, I don't know that. I couldn't really see, but I think he had glasses on. Very nice glasses.

PO: ⁵ _____ (old)

MO: Oh, he was younger than me. He was probably about 60. But, really, he looked like a very nice man!

PO: That's fine. Thank you very much for your help, Mrs Ogden.

b 🎧 5.6 Listen and check.

Vocabulary

Parts of the body

11 Label the pictures with the words in the box.

ear knee eyebrow thumb finger neck
fingernail hand leg mouth ~~head~~ nose
shoulder foot elbow toe wrist arm

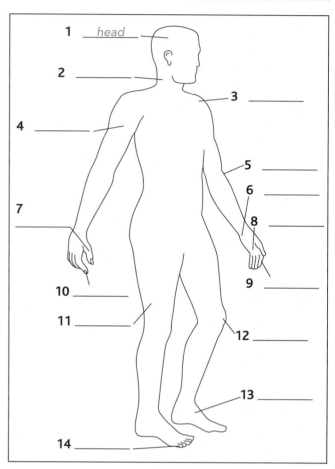

1 *head*
2 _____
3 _____
4 _____
5 _____
6 _____
7 _____
8 _____
9 _____
10 _____
11 _____
12 _____
13 _____
14 _____

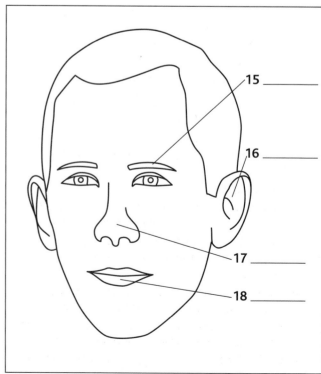

15 _____
16 _____
17 _____
18 _____

Vocabulary
Going on holiday

1a Anna is going on holiday. Look at the picture and tick (✓) the items in the box that she has remembered to pack. What has she forgotten?

passport   sun cream   sunglasses   guide book
swimsuit   phrase book   towel   credit cards
toothpaste   plane tickets   toothbrush
travel sickness pills   camera   foreign currency

b 🎧 6.1 Practise saying the words.

c Complete the sentences with words from exercise a.

1 I always take a _phrase book_ with me on holiday, and try to learn a few words in the local language.
2 It's better not to carry much _____ as you can pay for most things by credit or debit card.
3 I sometimes feel very ill on long journeys, so I always take _____ with me.
4 I remembered my toothbrush, but I didn't have any _____ , so I couldn't brush my teeth.
5 Check that you've got your passports and _____ before you leave home for the airport.
6 I always take one _____ to use on the beach, and a second one for the bathroom.
7 My brother always reads the _____ before we go to a place, so he knows where to visit.
8 If I don't wear _____ , my eyes often hurt.

Grammar focus 1
Plans and intentions

2 Make sentences about the Craven family using the prompts.

1 Rob and Sofia Craven live in England, but they / plan / move / to California.
   Rob and Sofia Craven live in England, but they
   are planning to move to California.
2 Rob is a cameraman and he / going / work / in a film studio there.
   _____
3 Sofia is a music teacher, but she / not / plan / work / for the first few months.
   _____
4 they / going / sell / their car, but they / not / going / sell their house. A friend of theirs / going / rent / it.
   _____
5 they've got a dog, Bruno, and they / plan / take / him with them.
   _____
6 in California, Sofia / like / buy / a house by the beach, but Rob / rather / have / an apartment with a big garden. The children / like / live / next door to Cameron Diaz!
   _____
7 Emily says she / like / have a horse, but Todd / rather / get / another dog.
   _____
8 Emily / like / learn / to ride, but Todd / rather / learn / to surf.
   _____

3 Write the questions for the answers about the Craven family.

1 *Where are they planning to move?*
To California.

2 _____
In a film studio.

3 _____
No, not for the first few months.

4 _____
Yes they are, but not their house.

5 _____
A friend of theirs.

6 _____
Yes, they are – they love Bruno.

7 _____
No, he'd rather have an apartment with a big garden.

8 _____
Next door to Cameron Diaz.

9 _____
A horse.

10 _____
He'd rather learn to surf.

4 Complete the article with the phrases in the box.

going to   he's   I would   planning to   not planning   I'm planning   is going   to retire   rather

SEEN AND HEARD

The best of this week's celebrity gossip
by Stella Renuzzi

Glamorous actress Sophie de Roy has said that she is in love with Argentinian dancer Hector Castagni. 'He's the perfect man for me,' she told me. 'It's not easy being a single girl, but I hope that's
¹ _going to_ change soon.' 'Sophie and I are both very young,' said Castagni in an interview with *KO* magazine. 'I would
² _____ wait for a few years before we make any important decisions. I'm ³ _____ to get married till I'm 30.'

Ex-footballer Jim Norton is in Hollywood, hoping for a career in films. And the good news for Jim is that he has found his first film role –
⁴ _____ going to play the part of 'Badger', a violent criminal, in the new Mo Amos film, *Gun Runner*. 'I don't think there's a big difference between acting and playing football,' he said to me, 'so I'm
⁵ _____ move here to help my film career.'

Angry that his last film *Smash!* did not win the Academy Award, film director Donald Braine has said that he's going ⁶ _____ from show business. 'If no one likes my films, that's not my problem,' he said. 'The film world is not important to me. I'm more interested in my new restaurant (also called Smash!).' And he has more news: '⁷ _____ to open another restaurant (Smash! 2) in Los Angeles next year,' he says.

Holly Pratelli, star of the TV soap opera *Hope Street*, ⁸ _____ to leave the series. She says it's because she doesn't like her new co-star, Chuck Ryder. 'I don't think he's handsome at all,' she told me. 'One day, ⁹ _____ like to have a big romantic scene with British actor Roy Thinn – he's gorgeous!'

Glossary
gossip = conversation or writing about other people's behaviour and private lives

Pronunciation
Contracted forms

5 🎧 6.2 Listen to the song titles and write *'d* or *'ll* in the gaps.

1 Who __*'ll*__ stop the rain? (Creedence Clearwater Revival)
2 I __*'d*__ wait for life (Take That)
3 It _____ be OK (Limp Bizkit)
4 I _____ hate to be you (She)
5 That _____ be the day (Buddy Holly)
6 Girl, you _____ be a woman soon (Urge Overkill)
7 You _____ be mine (The Pierces)
8 She _____ like to be in love (Kennedy Rose)
9 You _____ be surprised (Marilyn Monroe)
10 I _____ be waiting (Adele)
11 I just thought you _____ like to know (Johnny Cash)
12 You _____ always find me in the kitchen at parties (Jona Lewie)

Vocabulary
Describing holidays

6 Look at the phrases. Cross out one noun in each group which cannot go with the adjective.

	Adjective	Nouns
		~~passengers~~
1	crowded	train
		airport lounge
		hotel
2	comfortable	queue
		accommodation
		flight
3	long	scenery
		queue
		plane
4	peaceful	beach
		lake
		train
5	delayed	flight
		airport lounge
		holiday
6	luxurious	hotel
		lake

Grammar focus 2
Predictions with *will* and *won't*

7 Put *will* or *won't* in the correct place in the sentences.

1 It be difficult to find accommodation – there aren't many tourists at this time of year.
It won't be difficult to find accommodation – there aren't many tourists at this time of year.

2 Do you think we be able to buy tickets when we get there?
_____

3 I'm sorry, but there be any time for us to have lunch.
_____

4 You be all right if I go out for a couple of hours?
_____

5 I'm going to Michelle's party on Sunday. You be there, too?
_____

6 Don't worry. I'm sure there be any problems getting a visa.
_____

7 How long it take for us to get there?
_____

8 There be any food at your party?
_____

8a Complete the short answers.

1 **A:** Will Antonella be at the party on Friday?
B: Yes, _____*she will*_____ .
2 **A:** Will you say sorry?
B: No, _____ .
3 **A:** What do you think? Will it be a nice day?
B: Yes, _____ .
4 **A:** Will you be at home if I phone you at ten?
B: No, _____ .
5 **A:** Will you see Frank this afternoon?
B: Yes, _____ .
6 **A:** Will it take a long time to get to the airport?
B: No, _____ .
7 **A:** Will your parents be back this evening?
B: Yes, _____ .
8 **A:** Will I need sunglasses?
B: No, _____ .

b 🎧 6.3 Listen and check.

Language live

Making requests and asking for permission

9a Match the sentence halves.

1 Is it OK   `b`
2 Can you show
3 Could I have the
4 Can I have a ticket to
5 Do you mind bringing a
6 Do you mind if I take a photo

a of you?
b if I sit here?
c chicken, please?
d the airport, please?
e me your passport, please?
f towel to Room 267, please?

b Match sentences 1–6 in exercise a with the situations below.

Writing
An email

10a Look at the emails from two people who are on holiday. Who do you
think is enjoying the holiday more?

 New Message

Hi everyone,

Here we are in Delhi. It's a really interesting place, but it is boiling
(the average temperature is 35 degrees C). But our hotel is great – it's
really luxurious and there's a lovely swimming pool. I'm getting a nice
suntan. And we've had some tasty meals in the local restaurants.

Yesterday we went on a great excursion to see some famous places in
the city. There was a long queue to get in to the Red Fort, but it was
amazing!

I'll show you lots of pictures when I get back to the office next month.

Bye for now!

John

New Message

Dear Mario,

Your dad and I are having a short break in Scotland. Unfortunately,
our plane was delayed and the airline lost our suitcases! But it's all
OK now. We're staying in a very peaceful village called Plockton, in a
comfortable apartment by the sea.

Give our love to everyone,

Mum

PS I'm attaching a photo – as you can see, the weather is awful!

b What are they writing about? Write *yes* or *no*.

	accommodation	food	flight	weather
John	*yes*			
Mum				

c Now imagine that you are somewhere on holiday. Write an email to a
friend. Use some of the words and phrases in the box.

Hi   loads to do   Here we are   average temperature   quite cheap
Bye for now!   when I get home

Vocabulary

Verb phrases about ambitions

1 Complete the phrases with the correct verbs.

1 *go* round the world
   to university abroad

2 _____ to speak a foreign language
   how to fly a plane
   how to drive a car

3 _____ a degree
   married
   a job

4 _____ a millionaire
   good at something
   famous

5 _____ an interesting job
   children
   a large family

6 _____ a lot of money
   £100,000
   €250,000 a year

7 _____ a novel
   a book
   a computer program

8 _____ a house or flat
   a car
   a holiday home

Listen and read

Not always so successful

2a Read the article and choose the best title.

  A Not always so successful
  B How to be good at what you do
  C Three amazing achievements

These days, we know lots about the lives and the successes of famous people in sport, music and business. And perhaps we sometimes think that successful people have always been successful. Right? Well, let's have a look at some examples to see if that's true.

Sport – Michael Jordan

Michael Jordan is the greatest basketball player of all time. To many people, he has been ᴬ*a person who makes people want to do better.* His sporting achievements made him ᴮ*a very, very rich person.* But when he was at school, he lost his place on the school basketball team. And he went home and cried. His professional career has had failures as well as successes. He missed more than 9,000 shots in his career. As Jordan himself said, ¹_____

Music – Beethoven

During Beethoven's life, some people didn't think his music was very good. Beethoven's music teacher described him like this: ²_____ But Beethoven's ᶜ*hope* was to become a composer. He ᴰ*wanted to be very successful* and worked very hard all his life. And his music got better and better. Many people think he is the greatest composer of classical music ever.

Business – Soichiro Honda

As a young man, Soichiro Honda didn't have a job at all. He had ambition and lots of ideas for businesses, but they didn't work. He lost money and his wife had to sell her jewellery so that they had money for food. He tried to get a job with Toyota, but he didn't do very well at the interview. But he always had ᴱ*belief that he could do well.* In 1948, he ᶠ*opened a company* and now the Honda Motor Company has nearly 180,000 employees around the world. Soichiro Honda believed that when you have a problem or a failure, it can help you to learn and get better. He once said, ³_____

b Complete 1–3 in the article by putting the quotations below in the correct place.

A 'As a composer, he is hopeless.'
B 'Success is 99 percent failure.'
C 'I have lost almost 300 games. I have failed over and over and over again in my life. And that is why I succeed.'

c 🎧 7.1 Listen and check your answers to exercises a and b.

d Replace the phrases in italics (A–F) in the article with the words and phrases in the box.

....
dream   confidence   an inspiration   set his goals high
a multimillionaire   started his own business
....

A _____
B _____
C _____
D _____
E _____
F _____

Grammar focus 1

Present perfect and Past simple with *for*

3a Look at the grid below and find 21 more irregular past participles. Write the past participle and the base form in the table on the right.

H	E	A	R	D	R	B	S	A	T	C
M	A	D	E	O	U	R	E	K	S	O
W	T	O	L	D	N	O	E	T	P	M
R	E	S	O	L	D	U	N	C	O	E
I	N	E	S	U	N	G	F	O	K	D
T	P	U	T	N	C	H	O	S	E	N
T	D	R	U	N	K	T	U	T	N	T
E	G	O	T	G	W	O	N	Y	C	S
N	D	F	Y	P	A	I	D	D	A	W

Past participle	Base form
heard	*hear*
_____	_____
_____	_____
_____	_____
_____	_____
_____	_____
_____	_____
_____	_____
_____	_____
_____	_____
_____	_____
_____	_____
_____	_____
_____	_____
_____	_____
_____	_____
_____	_____
_____	_____
_____	_____
_____	_____
_____	_____
_____	_____

b 🎧 7.2 Listen and check. Practise saying the past participles.

4 Complete the sentences with the Present perfect form of the verbs in brackets.

1 We ___*have had*___ (have) our car for three years.
2 How long _____ (you / live) in London?
3 We _____ (not see) Amy for months.
4 Mike and Crystal _____ (be) married for about ten years.
5 There _____ (not be) anything good on TV for ages!
6 _____ (you / know) Bill for a long time?
7 How long _____ (you / be) interested in motorbikes?
8 I _____ (not wash) my car for two months!

5a Complete the article about Cher with the Present perfect or Past simple form of the verbs in brackets.

Few stars ¹___have had___ (have) careers as long and varied as Cher. In her career, she ²_____ (be) successful both as a singer and as an actress.

Born Cherilyn Sarkisian LaPiere in El Centro, California, on 20th May 1946, she ³_____ (leave) home for Hollywood at the age of 16. When she was only 17, she ⁴_____ (marry) songwriter and record producer Sonny Bono. As Sonny and Cher, they ⁵_____ (have) several hits in the 1960s, including *I Got You Babe* in 1964. But in the 1970s, success ⁶_____ (not be) so easy to find, and Cher and Sonny ⁷_____ (get) divorced in 1975. Soon after, Cher ⁸_____ (marry) rock star Gregg Allman, but the marriage ⁹_____ (not last) very long.

Since the mid-80s, Cher ¹⁰_____ (have) a second career as an actress, appearing in films like *The Witches of Eastwick* and *Faithful*. In 1988, she ¹¹_____ (win) a Best Actress Academy Award for the film *Moonstruck*.

More recently, Cher ¹²_____ (return) to singing once more, and with great success. Her single *Believe* ¹³_____ (become) US Number One in March 1999. In 2002, Cher ¹⁴_____ (start) a 'farewell tour', which ¹⁵_____ (last) for over two years! But even after that, she ¹⁶_____ (not stop) and from 2008 until 2011, she ¹⁷_____ (perform) at Caesar's Palace in Las Vegas. In 2011, she ¹⁸_____ (start) work on her 26th album. Since the 1960s, she ¹⁹_____ (sell) over 128 million albums worldwide. Her career ²⁰_____ (last) half a century and still ²¹_____ (not finish).

b 🎧 7.3 Listen and check.

6 Complete the sentences with the words in the box. Use each word twice.

....
‾ve   's   have   has   haven't   hasn't
....

1 A: I ¹___'ve___ just seen a friend of mine on TV. ²_____ you ever appeared on television?
   B: No, but my brother ³_____. He was in a video a few years ago.
   A: Really? Was it good?
   B: I don't know. I ⁴_____ seen it!
2 My friend Florence ⁵_____ always wanted to be a successful writer. She ⁶_____ written four novels, but she ⁷_____ made much money. I ⁸_____ read any of them myself, but she tells me they're very exciting.
3 The Diamante Brothers ⁹_____ been famous for more than 20 years. 'A show business life is the only life I ¹⁰_____ known,' says Dion Diamante. 'It ¹¹_____ been easy for us to live a normal life. But it ¹²_____ been a fantastic life so far!'

7 Choose the correct answers.

1 The Earth **existed** / **has existed** for more than 4,000 million years.
2 Dinosaurs **have lived** / **lived** on Earth for 160 million years.
3 Humans **have been** / **were** on the planet for just 50,000 years.
4 In the past, people **thought** / **have thought** that the world was flat.
5 The first Australians, the Aborigines, **have lived** / **lived** there for about 40,000 years.
6 For many years, the USA **has been** / **was** a British colony.
7 The USA **has been** / **was** an independent country for over 200 years.

Pronunciation

for and *have* in connected speech

8 🎧 7.4 Listen to the sentences and think about the pronunciation of the underlined words. One is stressed and one is unstressed. Write *S* (stressed) or *U* (unstressed) for each word.

1 <u>For</u> six years, he lived in <u>Brazil</u>. _U_ _S_

2 How long <u>have</u> you had that <u>car</u>? ____ ____

3 <u>Have</u> you <u>known</u> him for long? ____ ____

4 I <u>didn't</u> have a phone <u>for</u> three days last week. ____ ____

5 We've been <u>married</u> now <u>for</u> a year. ____ ____

6 How long <u>have</u> they been on <u>holiday</u>? ____ ____

Grammar focus 2

Present perfect and Past simple with other time words

9a Put *just*, *already*, *yet* or *never* in the correct place in the 'B' sentences.

1 **A:** What's the difference between Great Britain and the UK?

   B: I've told you twice!

   I've already told you twice! _____

2 **A:** Why are you looking so happy?

   B: I've heard that my cousin is coming to stay!

   _____

3 **A:** Would you like to go and see the new James Bond film tonight?

   B: Not really, I've seen it twice.

   _____

4 **A:** Is Ernesto here?

   B: No, he hasn't arrived.

   _____

5 **A:** Do you like Thai food?

   B: I don't know. I've tried it.

   _____

b 🎧 7.5 Listen and check. Practise saying the sentences.

10 Choose the correct answers.

1 My sister *just has bought / (has just bought)* a new computer.

2 Christine and Keith moved *last year to Canada / to Canada last year*.

3 I *have never been / never have been* abroad.

4 Have you had *anything to eat this morning / this morning anything to eat*?

5 I've heard a lot about Daniel, but I haven't met *yet him / him yet*.

6 We've *already seen / seen already* this film.

7 Have you heard the news? Andy and Samatha *have just got / just have got* engaged.

8 We've received *so far twenty-five emails / twenty-five emails so far*.

9 Mr and Mrs Wilson have lived *here for ten years / for ten years here*.

10 Have you *yet had lunch / had lunch yet*?

11 Choose one of the options in brackets to complete each sentence.

1 (already, yet, yesterday)
   We haven't told Laura about the accident
   _____yet_____ .

2 (went, gone, have gone)
   We _____ on a tour of central Africa last year.

3 (last night, yet, already)
   Didn't you finish your essay _____ ?

4 (yesterday, on Monday, so far)
   We've only visited two museums _____ .

5 (yet, ever, yesterday)
   I didn't see Keith _____ .

6 (just had, have just had, just have had)
   I'm afraid we _____ some bad news.

7 (today, yesterday, yesterday evening)
   You haven't done any work _____ .

4 Choose the correct answers.

1 a 'Where's **coffee** / **the coffee**?' 'It's in the cupboard on the left.'

b I always drink **coffee** / **the coffee** at breakfast time.

2 a **Swiss people** / **The Swiss people** all learn two languages at school.

b **The Swiss people** / **Swiss people** in my class all speak German.

3 a These days, it's easy to buy **books** / **the books** over the internet.

b Where are **books** / **the books** you borrowed from the library?

4 a What's **weather** / **the weather** like today?

b Some people think that people work harder in **cold weather** / **the cold weather**.

5 a Can you pass me **salt** / **the salt**, please?

b **Salt** / **The salt** is bad for you if you eat too much of it.

6 a This river is so polluted that all **fish** / **the fish** have died.

b Eating **fish** / **the fish** is very good for your heart.

7 a I went to see *Chicago* last night. **Music** / **The music** was great!

b I sometimes listen to **music** / **the music** when I'm working.

8 a I never borrow **money** / **the money** from friends.

b Have you already spent **money** / **the money** he gave you?

9 a Jenny is writing an article about **computers** / **the computers** for her school magazine.

b **Computers** / **The computers** in this room are available to all students between 9 a.m. and 6 p.m.

10 a I'll walk **dogs** / **the dogs** if you do the washing-up after dinner.

b Is it true that **dogs** / **the dogs** can only see in black and white?

5 Complete the fact file about Japan with *the* or –.

○ ○ ○

JAPAN: FACT FILE

¹___–___ Japan is not one island, but a group of over a thousand islands in ²_____ Pacific Ocean, in the east of ³_____ Asia. The four largest islands are ⁴_____ Hokkaido, ⁵_____ Honshu, ⁶_____ Kyushu and ⁷_____ Shikoku. Japan's nearest neighbours are ⁸_____ North and South Korea across ⁹_____ Sea of Japan, ¹⁰_____ China and ¹¹_____ Russian Federation. There are a number of volcanic mountains, including ¹²_____ Mount Fuji and ¹³_____ Mount Aso. Other important mountain ranges are ¹⁴_____ Chukogu Mountains and ¹⁵_____ Japanese Alps, not far from ¹⁶_____ Nagoya, the third city. Hokkaido is the furthest north of the main islands. The main city is ¹⁷_____ Sapporo on ¹⁸_____ River Ishikari. Popular holiday places are ¹⁹_____ Kitami Mountains and ²⁰_____ Lake Kussharo.

6 Complete the text with *a/an*, *the* or –.

I travel a lot on business. Last year I went to Abuja, ¹ *the* capital of ²_____ Nigeria. And that is where I saw ³_____ most amazing building I have ever seen: ⁴_____ house that looks like ⁵_____ aeroplane! It is ⁶_____ home of ⁷_____ couple from Lebanon, Liza and Jammal Said. Liza has always loved ⁸_____ travelling, so when she and Jammal got married, he promised to build her ⁹_____ house in the shape of ¹⁰_____ plane. In 1999, they heard that ¹¹_____ piece of land in Abuja was for sale. When they saw it, they knew it was ¹²_____ right place to build their dream home. ¹³_____ wings are 16 metres wide and ¹⁴_____ room in the cockpit is Liza and Jammal's office. From there, they have ¹⁵_____ lovely view of ¹⁶_____ city.

Vocabulary
Geographical features

7a Look at the grid below and find eleven more words about geographical features.

M	I	E	N	E	S	V
O	S	B	N	A	E	A
U	L	E	H	I	L	L
N	A	A	R	M	O	L
T	N	C	D	L	R	E
A	D	H	C	A	M	Y
I	S	N	O	N	O	S
N	R	O	A	T	U	L
R	I	C	S	R	N	D
A	V	E	T	E	T	E
N	E	A	S	E	A	S
G	R	N	T	L	I	E
E	S	S	S	L	N	R
S	F	O	R	E	S	T

b Match the descriptions with the words from exercise a.

1 They can be big or small; Ireland is one; they have water all around them. ___islands___
2 It's the land close to the sea; it can be rocky. _____
3 They are very high hills and often have rocks at the top; Everest is one. _____
4 They cover a lot of space; they can divide countries; for example, the Himalayas. _____
5 It's a large area of sand; for example, the Sahara. _____
6 It's a sandy place next to the sea; people often go there to swim and sunbathe. _____
7 Bridges go over them; fish live in them; they always go to the sea. _____
8 They are large seas and there are five in the world: the Arctic, the Antarctic, the Pacific, the Atlantic and the Indian. _____
9 They are areas of low land between hills; they often have a river in them. _____
10 It's a large area with lots of trees. _____
11 It's a large area of salt water; it's smaller than an ocean. _____
12 It's an area of high land, but smaller than a mountain. _____

Pronunciation
The letter *i*

8a The letter *i* can be pronounced: /ɪ/ as in *big* or /aɪ/ as in *microwave*. How do we pronounce the *i* in these words?

1 file _/aɪ/_
2 traditional _____
3 nightmare _____
4 credit _____
5 definitely _____
6 mind _____
7 online _____
8 decision _____
9 mobile _____
10 equipment _____
11 might _____
12 electric _____

b 🎧 8.1 Listen and check.

c Listen again and practise saying the words.

Grammar focus 2
Quantifiers with countable and uncountable nouns

9 Complete the sentences with *some*, *any* or *no*.

1 Helga can't work abroad because she doesn't speak ___any___ foreign languages.
2 Would you like _____ more coffee before you leave?
3 There are _____ letters for you over there, on the table.
4 Do you have _____ questions you'd like to ask me before we continue?
5 If there are _____ more questions, we can finish now.
6 I'm afraid there's _____ ice cream in the fridge. How about _____ fruit instead?
7 Can you buy _____ bread when you go to the supermarket?
8 I can't get a ticket from the machine – I haven't got _____ change.
9 There are _____ food shops open in the village on a Sunday, so you'll have to eat in a restaurant.
10 I can't do this now. I've got _____ time.

10a Look at the picture of Luke's bedroom. Complete the sentences with the words in the box.

much (x2) many a lot (x2) few no any

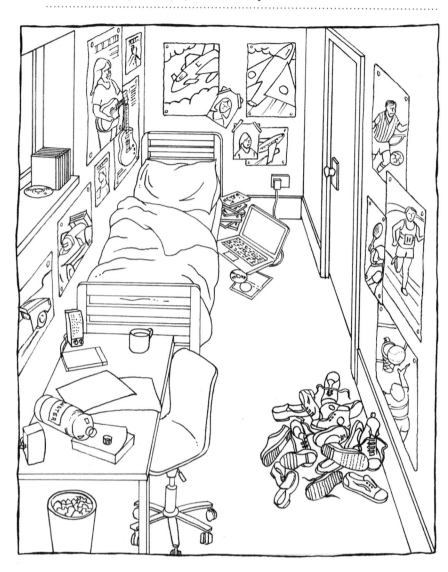

1 There isn't ___much___ space in his bedroom.
2 He hasn't got _____ books.
3 There are _____ of pictures on the walls.
4 There isn't _____ water in the bottle.
5 He's got _____ of tidying up to do!
6 There are _____ plants in his room.
7 He hasn't got _____ furniture in his room.
8 He's got a _____ computer games.

b 🎧 8.2 Listen and check. Practise saying the sentences.

11a Complete the sentences with *much, many, too much, too many* or *enough*.

1 I don't have very ___much___ free time during the week.
2 I know that I eat _____ chocolate and _____ cakes.
3 I don't usually do _____ exercise – unless I have to run for the bus!
4 I feel really tired because I didn't have _____ sleep last night.
5 I don't know _____ people who speak English well.
6 I don't have _____ money to go on holiday this year, so I'll have to stay at home.
7 I've got _____ things to do today. I won't be able to do them all.
8 I don't like coffee which has _____ sugar in it.
9 There aren't _____ shops near my house.
10 I don't think I've made _____ mistakes in this exercise!

b Which sentences are true for you?

12 Choose the correct answers.

1 My cousin is staying with us for *(a few)* / *a lot* days.
2 Hurry up! We haven't got *many* / *much* time.
3 Oh dear! I ate *too many* / *enough* chocolate biscuits and now I feel sick.
4 Have you had *a lot* / *enough* fruit juice or would you like some more?
5 There hasn't been *many* / *much* sunny weather this month.
6 I don't think we've got *any* / *no* bananas. I'll go and buy some more.
7 I don't watch *many* / *much* sport on TV.
8 You probably spend *too many* / *too much* time in front of your computer.
9 There are *any* / *no* books in this box – it's empty.
10 They've gone shopping. They want to buy *a few* / *any* presents for their friends.

Language live
Asking for and giving directions

13 There are two prepositions missing from each conversation. Complete the conversations by writing the words in the correct place.

of   to (x4)   on (x3)   for   at (x2)   down

1 A: Excuse me, can you help me, please? Where is the train station?
   B: Sure, no problem. Go *to*ₓ the end of this road. Go past the park. It's *on*ₓ your left.
   A: Great! Thank you.
2 A: Can you help me, please? I'm a bit lost. I'm looking a bank. But I can't find one.
   B: It's there, on the other side the road.
3 A: Sorry, where's the Filmland Cinema, please?
   B: Turn right the traffic lights here, then walk about 50 metres, and it's the corner.
4 A: Do you know where Keith's house is?
   B: Sure – it's near my dad's office. Walk West Street. When you come the traffic lights, turn left. It's the second house on your right.
5 A: Can you help us, please? We're looking for the President Hotel.
   B: Certainly. Go the end of this road and take the second right. Go past the cinema. It's the grey building your left.
6 A: Excuse me, can you help me, please? Where is the Natural History Museum?
   B: Go straight on the traffic lights, then take the first left. Its next the Grand Hotel.

Writing
Directions

14 Tomaso has invited his friend Jack to visit him for the weekend. Look at the map and complete Tomaso's email.

New Message

To: Jack jack_398@smellygreenfish.com
Subject: How to find my house
From: Tomaso tomasodegusto@yslb.co.uk

Hi Jack,

I'm happy you can come and stay next weekend. I'm sorry to hear your car's not working. Don't worry – it's very easy by public transport. From London Victoria Station, ¹ *take the train* to Beechen. You save money if you ² _____ online before you travel. It's about 45 minutes to Beechen. When you leave the railway station, the bus station is ³ _____ .

You need to catch the number 20 bus and ⁴ _____ at City Park (it's a ten-minute ride). Then walk down Park Road. It's a lovely park – ⁵ _____ .

You come to some traffic lights. ⁶ _____ and take the second right. That's Ocean Street, where I live. And my house is ⁷ _____ just before Valley Road.

See you then,

Tomaso

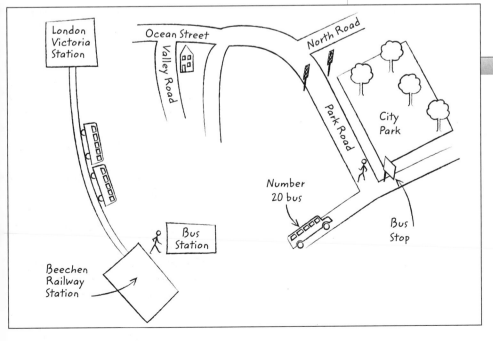

Listen and read

tonystravelshop.com

1a 🎧 **9.1 Listen and read. Answer the questions.**

Which product:
1 helps you use the internet?

_____

2 keeps you clean on a journey?

_____

3 makes you comfortable in hot weather?

_____

○ ○ ○

WWW.TONYSTRAVELSHOP.COM

Are you going on holiday soon? Then here are some great ideas for things you might need. And you can get them all right here on www.tonystravelshop.com.
Have a look and see what other visitors to www.tonystravelshop.com think.

AIR-CONDITIONED SHIRT

Are you going somewhere really hot on your holiday? Wait a minute – the air conditioning in your hotel might not work! You'll get really hot and everyone knows that you can't enjoy yourself if you're too hot. But don't worry: with this amazing air-conditioned shirt, you'll be cool and comfortable. It's got a small air-conditioner with a fan under the arm at the back.

£159   Click here for more info.

PERSONALISED AIRLINE SEAT COVER

Millions of people travel by plane each year. This means that lots of people sit in every airline seat. Just think how dirty the seat gets! But with this fantastic personalised airline seat cover, you won't have to worry about dirty uncomfortable seats again. Just put the cover on your seat when you get on the plane. Enjoy your flight!

From just £29   Click here for more info.

WIFI NETWORK DETECTOR T-SHIRT

Are you worried that you won't have a very good internet connection on your holiday? Then you need the Wifi Network Detector T-shirt. It uses batteries and will tell you how strong the wifi signal is. Use it in your hotel, at the airport, even on the beach!

Only £30   Click here for more info.

b **Look at some user reviews on www.tonystravelshop.com. Which product are they describing?**

1 Yes, and I think all the other passengers will want one, too!
Homeboy, Washington DC, USA

2 But won't the fan make a noise? And who wants noisy clothes?
Pierre, Lyon, France

3 I've got one. And I'll never fly again without it. It's brilliant!
Ali, Dubai

4 Do the lights flash when the signal is good? Great idea!
Buppha, Thailand

5 It may make you a bit cooler, but not much, I don't think.
Mark, Moscow

6 My internet signal isn't very good in all the rooms in my home. I think it'll be helpful in the home, but not on holiday.
Greenleaves, Hong Kong

7 But will they let you use it in a plane? I don't think so!
Moondragon, Venezuela

Vocabulary
Modern equipment

2 Match the sentence halves.

1 If you cook food in a microwave ⟦d⟧
2 It's so hot in my country that we have the air ☐
3 I think my vacuum ☐
4 She's got a really big flat- ☐
5 My internet provider is sending me a new wifi ☐
6 My great grandmother never had a washing ☐
7 It's really cold in my flat because the central ☐

a heating isn't working.
b cleaner needs a new bag.
c conditioning on all the time.
d oven, it never tastes as good.
e screen television on her sitting room wall.
f router because the old one is always very slow.
g machine – she washed all her family's clothes by hand.

3 Complete the sentences with the words in the box.

> freezer   shower   fridge   oven   ~~computer~~   dishwasher

1 I lost all my photos when my   _computer_   crashed last week.
2 The temperature inside a _____ is between -16 and -24°C.
3 I like to roast meat slowly in the _____ .
4 Before I bought my _____ , I spent about half an hour every day washing the dishes by hand.
5 I didn't like the flat because the bathroom had a bath, but no _____ .
6 Is there any milk in the _____ ?

Pronunciation
Stress patterns in compound nouns

4a Think about the stress in these compound nouns. Is the stress on the first word or the second? Put them in the right group.

> air conditioning   central heating   vacuum cleaner
> washing machine   microwave oven

Oo (stress on the first word)	oO (stress on the second word)

b 🎧 9.2 Listen and check.

Grammar focus 1
may, *might*, *will definitely*, etc.

5a On 31st December 2012, Madame Sol, a famous astrologer, made some predictions for the next ten years. Write out the sentences using *will* or *won't*.

1 there / be / a woman president of the United States
   There will be a woman president of the United States.
2 China / be / the world's richest country
   _____
   _____
   _____
3 astronauts / visit / the planet Mars
   _____
   _____
4 people / not use / cash. / they / only / use / credit cards
   _____
   _____
   _____
5 there / be / no more living elephants
   _____
   _____
   _____
6 people / not buy / TVs. / they / only / watch / programmes online
   _____
   _____
   _____

b Write some predictions of your own about the next ten years, using the ideas in the sentences in exercise a.

1 *There won't be a woman president in my country in the next ten years.*

2 _____

3 _____

4 _____

5 _____

6 _____

6 Match the sentence halves.

1 My mobile's broken, so I'll ☐ d
2 On the weather forecast, they said it'll ☐
3 I've applied for a brilliant job, but I probably ☐
4 She's going to a party tonight, but she probably ☐
5 Hi, I'm ringing to say I had to stay longer at work today, so I'll ☐
6 They didn't really enjoy their holiday and they said they probably ☐

a won't get it.
b probably rain tomorrow.
c won't go there again.
d probably buy a new one.
e probably get home a bit late tonight. Bye.
f won't stay long – she has to get up early tomorrow.

7 Put the words in the correct order to make sentences.

1 will / win / probably / I / Germany / think / the football match.
   I think Germany will probably win the football match.

2 be / There / won't / any / tonight / snow / definitely
   _____

3 will / tomorrow / be / Stefan / definitely / at home
   _____

4 the answer / know / probably / to your question / won't / He
   _____

5 able / will / We / next week / be / to give / you / definitely / an answer
   _____

8 Rewrite the sentences replacing the phrase in bold with *may* (*not*) or *might* (*not*).

1 **It's possible that** Martin **will** be at Sally's party on Saturday.
   Martin may/might be at Sally's party on Saturday.

2 **Maybe** we **will** go abroad for our holidays next year.
   _____

3 **Perhaps** they **won't** be able to finish the work until next week.
   _____

4 **It's possible that** it **will** get cold later.
   _____

5 **Maybe** she **won't** want to go out this evening.
   _____

6 **Perhaps** Martha **will not** be able to help you.
   _____

7 **Maybe** the Prime Minister **will** resign if things don't get better.
   _____

8 Buy a lottery ticket; **it's possible that** you'll win £1 million!
   _____

9a Rob is a builder. He has just bought a house and is showing it to his friend Adam. Complete their conversation with sentences a–h.

a   I'll probably get a completely new kitchen
b   We may not move in this year.
c   We might have a wooden floor
d   I'll definitely buy a new boiler.
e   We'll probably have carpets
f   Well, we definitely won't do that!
g   I'll definitely put some new ones in.
h   it may be too expensive

A: So, this is your new house? It looks great! When are you moving in?

R: Well, there's a lot of building work to do first. ¹_b_

A: Why? You've got the keys – you could move in tomorrow!

R: ²_ I mean, look at the house – the windows are broken.

A: Hmm … yes. What are you going to do about them?

R: ³_

A: Right.

R: And inside the house, all the rooms are in a bad state. That's why we bought the house very cheaply.

A: So, what else are you going to do to the house?

R: ⁴_ : new cooker, fridge, dishwasher, washing machine … It won't be cheap!

A: True.

R: In fact, ⁵_ , so perhaps we'll keep the old kitchen for now. We haven't decided yet.

A: Yes, you need to do the most important things first.

R: That's right. ⁶_ . The old one's completely broken, so there's no hot water.

A: And what will the house be like inside?

R: It'll be comfortable, I hope. ⁷_ in all the rooms.

A: Really? But wooden floors look very nice.

R: True. ⁸_ in the sitting room. But it depends on my wife. She's the boss – I just do all the work!

b   🎧 **9.3** Listen and check.

10a Read the daily horoscope and answer the questions.

Which sign

1   may have family problems? _Cancer_
2   will have a good day at school? _____
3   may need more money than usual? _____
4   will have more things to do than usual? _____
5   may get very angry? _____

★★ **astrology.com** ★★

← **YESTERDAY** | **TOMORROW** →

Send this horoscope to a friend ✉

Your daily horoscope for
Wednesday 17th May
by Sylvia Fox

Taurus
You might have an argument with an important person today. If this happens, you'll need help. A friend or partner will be very useful to you. And who knows? You might win the argument!

Gemini
This will be another busy work day for you: you'll have all the normal things to do, but there may also be an extra job or two. But don't worry, you'll succeed! And think how happy you'll be when you finish!

Cancer
You may have to choose between your public and your private life today. You won't spend much time with your loved ones until later in the week. Make sure they know you love them or they may feel forgotten.

Leo
This will be your lucky day for education! If you're still at school, it'll be a good day for study – something you've always thought was too hard for you will be easy. If you've already left school, think about going back to your studies – you won't regret it!

Virgo
There will be some money worries today. Check what you're spending. You may need to spend some extra money on travel, but if you buy something for a loved one, they may not thank you for it!

b   Underline all the examples of predictions in the text.

c   🎧 **9.4** Listen to some of the predictions. Practise saying the sentences.

Vocabulary
Adjectives for describing places

11a Look at the grid below and find 13 more adjectives for describing places.

B	O	L	D	F	A	S	H	I	O	N	E	D
L	A	R	G	E	T	A	S	P	C	H	E	A
O	M	A	D	E	T	O	P	E	I	S	R	R
C	O	M	F	O	R	T	A	B	L	E	S	K
O	D	E	L	E	A	M	C	H	O	R	S	E
D	E	P	I	T	C	L	I	G	H	T	H	E
P	R	I	V	A	T	E	O	M	A	T	A	S
I	N	T	E	R	I	S	U	L	L	O	D	S
S	M	A	L	L	V	O	S	U	N	N	Y	T
I	S	L	Y	M	E	T	O	Q	U	I	E	T

b Write the words from the grid in the correct place below.

Across
1 big: _____
2 not modern or fashionable: _____
3 A _____ place is one where you can be alone.
4 not large: _____
5 If something is _____ , it makes you feel physically relaxed.
6 A _____ room is full of sunlight (the first letter is 'l').
7 A _____ garden or room is full of sunlight (the first letter is 's').
8 A _____ place doesn't have much activity or many people.

Down
9 full of activity: _____
10 nice to look at: _____
11 A _____ room has lots of space.
12 A _____ house doesn't have much light.
13 A _____ garden is away from the direct heat and light of the sun.
14 A _____ building or room is in a new style or has new equipment.

Grammar focus 2
Present tense after *if*, *when* and other time words

12 Match the sentence halves and use the prompts to write conditional sentences.

1 if the weather / be / good this weekend,   [e]
2 if you / work / hard,   ☐
3 if you / be / late for class again,   ☐
4 if you / not get up / soon,   ☐
5 if the train / arrive / on time,   ☐
6 if you / not take / a map,   ☐
7 if we / see / a restaurant,   ☐

a you / pass / all your exams
b we / be / home before midnight
c you / get / lost
d your teacher / get / very annoyed
e we / have / a barbecue
f we / stop / for lunch
g you / be / late for class

1 *If the weather's good this weekend, we'll have a barbecue.*
2 _____
3 _____
4 _____
5 _____
6 _____
7 _____

13 Choose the correct answers.

1 I'll call you **as soon as** / **before** / **if** I arrive.
2 **As soon as** / **If** / **When** you don't leave me alone, I'll call the police!
3 What are you going to do **as soon as** / **if** / **when** you finish university?
4 If we drive quickly, we'll probably get home **before** / **if** / **when** it gets dark.
5 This exam is very important for Kim. **As soon as** / **If** / **When** she passes, she can go to university.
6 Please check you have all your luggage **as soon as** / **If** / **When** you leave the train.
7 **As soon as** / **Before** / **If** you go, could you give me your email address?
8 Promise to tell me the news **as soon as** / **before** / **if** you hear anything.
9 I'm sure I'll be married **as soon as** / **if** / **when** I'm 30.

10 TAKE CARE!

Vocabulary
Accidents and injuries

1 Complete the sentences with the words in the box.

....
allergic   breathless   ~~burn~~   come round   faints   plaster
rash   sting   swollen   cream
....

1 Be careful not to __burn__ yourself when you use the iron.
2 Has anyone got a _____ ? I've cut my finger.
3 My mum always _____ when she sees a spider. Last time I had to throw a bucket of water at her to make her _____ .
4 The doctor gave me some _____ to put on my skin.
5 I get _____ quickly when I run, so I have to stop and rest.
6 I think I'm _____ to the washing powder. I've got this horrible _____ all over my back.
7 Where exactly did the bee _____ you? I can't see anything.
8 I hit my finger with a hammer and now it's _____ . It's really big and it hurts.

Grammar focus 1
Past continuous

2 Complete the sentences with the Past continuous form of the verbs in brackets.

When SS *Titanic* hit the iceberg,
1 people __were dancing__ (dance) in the ballroom.
2 the captain _____ (read) a book in his cabin.

When John Lennon met Paul McCartney,
3 John _____ (play) with a group called The Quarrymen.
4 rock 'n' roll music _____ (become) popular in England.

When Neil Armstrong first walked on the moon,
5 the other astronauts _____ (sit) inside Apollo 11.
6 millions of people _____ (watch) it on television.

When Nelson Mandela left prison,
7 his wife Winnie _____ (wait) for him.
8 his supporters _____ (sing) outside the prison.

3a Complete the conversation with the Past continuous form of the verbs in brackets or with short answers.

PO = Police Officer   **MA** = Mr Adams

PO: Now, Mr Adams , what [1]__were you doing__ (you / do) between 7 and 9 p.m. last night?
MA: I [2]_____ (watch) a film at the cinema.
PO: [3]_____ (your wife and children / watch) it with you?
MA: No, [4]_____ .
PO: What [5]_____ (they / do)?
MA: They [6]_____ (visit) my mother-in-law.
PO: I see. Now, [7]_____ (it / rain) when you went into the cinema?
MA: Yes, [8]_____ .
PO: [9]_____ (you / carry) an umbrella?
MA: No, [10]_____ .
PO: What about when you left the cinema? [11]_____ (it / rain) then?
MA: Yes. I mean, no, [12]_____ .
PO: And [13]_____ (your wife / wait) for you outside?
MA: No. No, [14]_____ .
PO: I think you're lying, Mr Adams. Someone saw you outside the cinema, in the rain, carrying an umbrella, with your wife. And it was 7:30 p.m.!

b 🎧 **10.1 Listen and check.**

4 Choose the correct answers.
1 We *saw* / *were seeing* Adam while we were waiting for the bus.
2 As I *got* / *was getting* ready for bed, my phone rang. It was Pete.
3 Tricia was swimming when she *lost* / *was losing* her watch.
4 Did it start raining while you *played* / *were playing* tennis this morning?
5 I *sat* / *was sitting* in front of the TV watching a documentary when I fell asleep.
6 I *cooked* / *was cooking* supper when I heard a knock on the door.
7 Where were you and Jamie living when you *got* / *were getting* married?
8 She *hurt* / *was hurting* her back while she was playing football.
9 Mick *fell* / *was falling* off the ladder when he was cleaning the windows.
10 We *cycled* / *we cycling* through the park when we heard a strange noise.

5a Complete the sentences with the Past simple or Past continuous form of the verbs in brackets.

1 I _was watching_ (watch) TV at home when someone ___came___ (come) to the door.
2 My mother _____ (come back) from work while I _____ (prepare) dinner.
3 When we _____ (arrive) home, some friends _____ (wait) for us.
4 When I _____ (wake up), everyone _____ (look) at me.
5 Jane _____ (see) another guest who _____ (wear) exactly the same hat!
6 We _____ (have) breakfast when the doorbell _____ (ring).
7 It _____ (begin) to rain while I _____ (wash) the car.
8 He _____ (study) for a test when his friend _____ (phone) him.
9 It _____ (not snow) when we _____ (leave) the house.
10 As I _____ (walk) along the street, I _____ (see) an old friend.

b 🎧 10.2 Listen and check. Practise saying the sentences.

6 Read the story of when Dave Mascott met his hero and complete it with the Past simple or Past continuous form of the verbs in brackets.

DAVE, YOU'VE GOT A VISITOR!

The famous American rock star Bob Goldhart [1] _was doing_ (do) a tour of Britain when he [2] _____ (meet) British rock star Dave Wells at a party. As he [3] _____ (leave), Dave [4] _____ (invite) Bob to come to his house and [5] _____ (tell) him the address. But Bob [6] _____ (made) a mistake as he [7] _____ (write) down the address: he wrote 'Addison Street' instead of 'Addison Road'.

The next day, Helen Mascott of 145 Addison Street, London, [8] _____ (listen) to the radio in her kitchen when the doorbell [9] _____ (ring). A man with long hair [10] _____ (stand) outside. She [11] _____ (think) the man [12] _____ (look) familiar, but [13] _____ (not say) anything. 'Is Dave in?' the man [14] _____ (ask) politely. The woman, whose husband's name was also Dave, [15] _____ (explain) that Dave [16] _____ (do) the shopping, but he would be back in a few minutes. She [17] _____ (invite) Bob Goldhart to come in and wait. While Helen [18] _____ (make) some coffee, he [19] _____ (look) around the living room and [20] _____ (be) very happy to see all of his albums!

A few minutes later, Dave [21] _____ (arrive) home. 'You've got a visitor,' Helen [22] _____ (tell) her husband. When Dave, a big, big fan of Bob Goldhart, [23] _____ (open) the living room door and [24] _____ (see) who [25] _____ (wait) for him, he [26] _____ (faint)!

Vocabulary

Feeling ill

7a Which person in the picture:

1 has got a fever? ☐
2 has got a toothache? ☐
3 has got a sore throat? ☐
4 has got cold? ☐
5 has got an earache? ☐
6 is going to be sick? ☐
7 has got a cough? ☐
8 has got a headache? ☐
9 keeps sneezing? ☐
10 has got a leg that hurts? ☐

7b Complete the sentences with the words in the box.

> sick coughing toothache sneeze cold fever sore throat headache hurts earache

1 Have you got a tissue? I think I'm going to _____.
2 I played tennis for two hours yesterday and now my arm _____.
3 My daughter feels very hot. I think she's got a _____.
4 My throat hurts because I can't stop _____.
5 I shouted a lot at the concert and now I've got a _____.
6 I can't hear very well because I've got an _____.
7 I've eaten too much and I think I'm going to be _____.
8 I got soaking wet yesterday and I think I'm getting a _____.
9 My mouth really hurts because I've got _____.
10 Can you turn the music down please because I've got a _____.

51

Grammar focus 2

used to

8 Roger lives with his wife and children in Scotland. He drives a Rolls Royce car, has a private plane and always wears expensive clothes. But things weren't always so good for Roger. Write six sentences with *used to* and the verbs in the box.

wear   have   be (x2)   work   live

1 (very unhappy)

He used to be very unhappy.

2 (old clothes)

3 (very boring job)

4 (hamburger restaurant)

5 (poor)

6 (on his own)

9 Write negative sentences about Roger with *used to* and the words in brackets.

1 (be / rich)

He didn't use to be rich.

2 (live / Scotland)

3 (drive / Rolls Royce)

4 (have / private plane)

5 (wear / designer clothes)

6 (have / a family)

10 Rewrite the sentences with *used to* where possible.

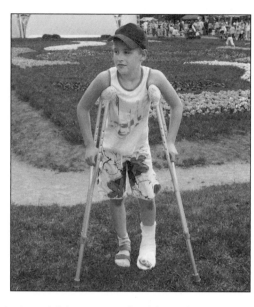

1 As a child I was very healthy. I didn't have many colds and I only went to hospital once, when I broke my leg.

As a child I was very healthy. I didn't use to have many colds and I only went to hospital once, when I broke my leg.

2 Claudia had a bicycle, but she sold it when her parents gave her a motorbike.

3 My little brother hated vegetables. He always put them on my plate when I wasn't looking!

4 Last weekend we stayed in a little hotel by the sea, where I stayed every year on family holidays.

5 There was a sweet shop on the corner of the street. I remember we bought sweets on the way home from school every day.

6 There weren't many fast food restaurants in this town 20 years ago. Now there are at least ten!

7 She worked in that shop many years ago. I saw her every day on my way to school.

Pronunciation
use(d) in connected speech

11 🎧 **10.3** Listen to the conversation. Is *use(d)* pronounced with /s/ or /z/?

A: How often do you ¹**use** a computer? _/z/_

B: I ²**use** mine every day. What about you? ____

A: Actually, I never ³**used** to have one. I only bought one this year. ____

B: Really? So how did you ⁴**use** to send emails and things? ____

A: Oh, easy. I just ⁵**used** my phone for those things.

____

Language live
Talking about health

12a Complete the conversation with the phrases in the box.

....

I have a nut allergy.   What can I do for you?
I get breathless   what are your symptoms?
Are you taking any medication?

....

Patient: Good morning, Doctor Chang.

Doctor: Good morning. ¹_____

Patient: Well, I wanted to see you because I'm not feeling very well.

Doctor: Right. And ²_____

Patient: Well, ³_____ very often.

Doctor: Is this when you do sport or run fast?

Patient: No, I don't do sport or run. It's when I'm at work.

Doctor: And are you allergic to anything?

Patient: Yes, ⁴_____ But I never have them, of course.

Doctor: No, of course not. ⁵_____

Patient: Yes, I take paracetamol.

Doctor: I see. Well, perhaps you shouldn't take it so often. And I think you need to relax more ...

b 🎧 **10.4** Listen and check.

Writing
Time words in a narrative

13 Use the notes to write the story. Use the Past simple and Past continuous.

* One day / as Gunther Hauser / drive down a road in Austria, / see a goat on the road

* Mr Hauser / stop the car / and wait. But the goat / not move

* Eventually, / he / get out of the car to move the goat

* Suddenly, / the goat / get up

* Before / he could shut the car door, / the goat / get into Mr Hauser's car

* The man / get back into the car / the goat / not get out

* When / he take a photo of the goat / it / eat the car seat!

* After some time, / the man / go to ask for help

* He walk / to the next house

* When / he arrive, / the people think Mr Hauser was a burglar

* Finally, / he telephone the police

* Eventually, / they get the goat out of the car!

Listen and read

Our top four hates

1a 🎧 **11.1 Read the article and put the headings (a–d) in the right place. Then listen and check.**

   a Slow internet
   b Poor customer service
   c People who eat with their mouth open
   d People who drive too close to the car in front

Our top four hates

Last week, we asked our readers to tell us about things they really hate. We've had a huge response – it's clear that there are lots of things that lots of people really do not like. Here are the top four.

1 _____

This annoys people more than anything else. We all know that roads can be dangerous places. And if cars get too close to each other, [1]**they** can be very dangerous places. Most drivers leave a sensible distance between their car and the car in front. But some don't. Why? Why? Why?

2 _____

Let's face it – we pay a lot to our phone networks and to our internet service providers. They always say they've got a super-fast connection. And if they're making us pay for [2]**it**, we should make them provide it.

3 _____

Come on, it's not really that difficult, is it? OK, babies aren't very good at it and their food goes all over the floor. But [3]**that** doesn't last very long and most people can eat nicely and politely by the time they're five or six. But there are SOME people who eat with their mouth open. Argh! Please don't – it's disgusting! We really don't want to see the food inside your mouth!

4 _____

Being polite to members of the public is important – and easy. It doesn't matter if [4]**it's** in a shop, in a restaurant or on the phone. Staff should always be nice and polite to the customer. And it's good business, too. We'll probably go back to a shop if the service was good. But if the staff were rude, we tell our friends. And then they don't go back either.

b Look at the words in bold in the article. What does the word refer to in each case?

1 they
   a people
   b roads
   c cars

2 it
   a internet bill
   b phone network
   c super-fast connection

3 that
   a eating nicely
   b food going on the floor
   c eating with the mouth open

4 it
   a good customer service
   b a phone
   c a shop

Vocabulary
Adjectives with dependent prepositions

2 Match the sentence halves.

1 She's keen ⬜ *i*
2 Life is so full ⬜
3 If I was good ⬜
4 I'm not interested ⬜
5 I'm really similar ⬜
6 He wasn't surprised ⬜
7 You shouldn't be worried ⬜
8 Lots of people are afraid ⬜
9 What kind of suncream is suitable ⬜
10 John is completely different ⬜

a of suprises.
b for babies' skin?
c in money, but I do think it's very useful!
d about it – everything will be fine!
e at singing, I'd join a choir.
f from me, but we are best friends.
g to my dad – we're both really tall.
h of the dark, but I don't understand why!
i on tennis, but doesn't have enough time to play very often.
j about doing so well in the exam, because he worked so hard.

Grammar focus 1
like and *would like*

3a Choose the correct answers.

1 What do you think Ian **would like** / **likes** for his birthday?
2 Annette **likes** / **would like** Brad Pitt so much she's got all his films on DVD.
3 **I'd like to speak** / **I like speaking** to Mr Shizuko, please.
4 **Would you like to go** / **Do you like going** for a coffee after class today?
5 One day, I **love going** / **would love to go** to Hawaii.
6 She always drives to college. She **doesn't like walking** / **wouldn't like to walk**.
7 It's late and **I'd like to go** / **I like going** home. Can you phone for a taxi?
8 Yes, I **would love to come** / **love coming** with you tomorrow.
9 My sister Christine **doesn't like** / **wouldn't like** pop music.
10 I **don't like getting up** / **wouldn't like to get up** early, so I prefer the night shift.
11 **I'd like to help** / **I like helping** you, but I'm afraid I can't.
12 I **would love to be** / **love being** a professional ballet dancer, but I'm too tall.

b 🎧 **11.2 Listen and check.**

4 Complete the sentences with the correct form of the verbs in brackets.

1 I'd like _to stay_ (stay), but I have to be back by 5 o'clock.
2 We're late! And Pete doesn't like _____ (wait)!
3 What would you like _____ (eat)?
4 Do you like _____ (go) to football matches or do you think it's better to watch them on TV?
5 We'd like _____ (buy) a car, but we haven't got much money at the moment.
6 Would you like _____ (come) with us?
7 I really don't like _____ (clean) the house, so I don't do it very often!
8 He's never really liked _____ (go) to parties.

5 Put the sentences in the correct order. Write the full text in the space below.

a My friends and I all like ☐ 1
b like to be a professional opera singer. I ☐
c singing (she's really good at it) and she'd ☐
d I'd like to do one of these subjects at university. ☐
e doing completely different things. Alice, my best friend, likes ☐ 2
f like listening to music in my free time, but I wouldn't like ☐
g start my own business, and I'm really interested in economics and finance. I think ☐
h to be a musician as a job. I'd be worried about money all the time! I'd really like to ☐

My friends and I all like doing completely different
things. Alice, my best friend, likes _____
_____
_____
_____
_____
_____
_____
_____
_____

Pronunciation
Intonation in invitations

6a 🎧 11.3 Listen to someone saying the invitations. You will hear each invitation twice. Which is friendlier: a or b?

1 Would you like to go to the cinema tomorrow? ☐
2 What would you like to drink? ☐
3 I'm having a party on Saturday – would you like to come? ☐
4 Where would you like to sit? ☐
5 Would you like to come and meet my parents next week? ☐

b Listen again. Practise saying the sentences.

Vocabulary
Survival items

7a Complete the words by adding the missing vowels.

1 t_o_rch	6 m_tch_s
2 t_nt	7 b_ttl_d w_t_r
3 bl_nk_t	8 kn_f_
4 c_mp_ss	9 r_p_
5 s_ncr__m	10 m_rr_r

b Which of the items in exercise a:

1 can you sleep in? _____
2 can you sleep under? _____
3 lets you start a fire? _____
4 shows you where north is? _____
5 helps you see in the dark? _____
6 protects your skin from the sun? _____
7 can you use to see your face? _____
8 can you drink? _____
9 is useful if you are climbing? _____
10 cuts food? _____

Grammar focus 2
Conditional sentences with *would*

8 Complete the sentences with the phrases in the box.

> was ~~would be~~ could sunbathe would you remember
> could go would you buy had would need could have
> would come won might lend

1 If I had a compass on my mobile phone, it
   ___would be___ really useful on holiday.
2 She says that if she _____ a better voice,
   she'd sing in a choir.
3 If you _____ £20,000 in the lottery, what
   would you spend it on?
4 If you had a pet, _____ to feed it?
5 We _____ blankets if the heating didn't
   work.
6 If we had some suncream, we _____ for
   longer.
7 If you had a million dollars, what _____ ?
8 If I _____ more interested in politics, I'd
   read a newspaper every day.
9 If I didn't have to stay at home tomorrow, I
   _____ with you.
10 If you asked John, he _____ you the
   money you need.
11 If it wasn't so cold, we _____ a picnic in
   the park.
12 If I _____ anywhere in the world, I'd
   spend a year on a desert island.

9 Complete the sentences with the correct form of the
verbs in brackets.

1 Would you go to his party if he ___invited___
   (invite) you?
2 I _____ (can / help) you translate this text
   into German if we had a dictionary.
3 We _____ (email) her if we had her
   address.
4 If I _____ (know) the answer, I wouldn't
   need to ask.
5 I'd probably buy a laptop if they _____ (be)
   cheaper.
6 Where would you live if you _____ (have)
   the choice?
7 If they _____ (make) a film of your life,
   which actor would play you?
8 If the rooms were bigger, we _____ (can /
   buy) larger furniture.

10 Complete the sentences with the correct form of the
verbs in brackets.

1 If you ___had___ (have) 20 brothers and
   sisters, think how many birthday presents you
   ___would get___ (get)!
2 If I _____ (not work), we _____
   (not have) enough money to live.
3 I'm sure you _____ (feel) better if you
   _____ (not get up) so late.
4 If we _____ (leave) early, we _____
   (visit) Janet on the way.
5 I don't know what I _____ (do) if you
   _____ (not be) here to help me.
6 If I _____ (have) a lot of money, I
   _____ (take) you on an expensive holiday.
7 If everyone _____ (speak) the same
   language, do you think life_____ (be)
   better?
8 I'm sorry, I don't know. If I _____ (know)
   the answer, I _____ (tell) you.

11a Match the sentence halves.

1 He might help you   `b`
2 She wouldn't go out with him   ☐
3 If I could go on holiday anywhere in the world, ☐
4 Robert might do better at school   ☐
5 If you told her the truth,   ☐
6 If you didn't drink so much coffee before
   going to bed,   ☐

a if he did his homework regularly.
b if you were more polite to him.
c she might get very angry.
d if he didn't have so much money.
e you might sleep better.
f I'd go to Florida.

b 🎧 11.4 Listen and check. Practise saying the
sentences.

12 Tick the correct sentence.

1 a If they didn't have to work, they would join us. ☑
  b If they wouldn't have to work, they joined us. ☐
2 a He might pass the test if he would work harder. ☐
  b He might pass the test if he worked harder. ☐
3 a If it was warmer, I will go for a swim. ☐
  b If it was warmer, I might go for a swim. ☐
4 a Would you tell me if you knew? ☐
  b Do you tell me if you knew? ☐
5 a If the pay was better, I'd accept the job. ☐
  b If the pay would be better, I'd accept the job. ☐
6 a It would be great if the kitchen was tidier. ☐
  b It was great if the kitchen would be tidier. ☐
7 a I sold my car if it wouldn't be so old. ☐
  b I would sell my car if it wasn't so old. ☐

13a Write questions with *if* and *would* using the prompts.

1 what / you / do / you / be / prime minister / for a
week?

What would you do if you were prime minister for
a week?

2 who / you / meet / you / can / meet / any famous
person?

_____

3 you / can / live / forever / you / want to?

_____

4 what / you / buy / you / have / 1,000,000 euros?

_____

5 where / you / live / you / can / live / anywhere in
the world?

_____

6 you / lose / your mobile / it / be / a problem?

_____

7 you / can / live / your life again / what / you /
change?

_____

8 it / rain / every day for a year / what / you / do?

_____

b Answer the questions in exercise a. Write full
answers.

1 *If I was prime minister for a week, I would give*
everyone a day off!
2 _____
_____
3 _____
_____
4 _____
_____
5 _____
_____
6 _____
_____
7 _____
_____
8 _____
_____

12 BRAND NEW

Vocabulary
Types of product

1a Match words 1–5 with words a–e to make phrases.

1 electronic ☐
2 soft ☐
3 internet search ☐
4 fast ☐
5 chocolate ☐

a bars
b food
c engine
d drink
e goods

b Complete the sentences with phrases from exercise a.

1 I never eat _____ – it's got too much sugar and salt, and I don't like it.
2 It's healthier to have a glass of water than a can of _____ .
3 Yesterday I was so hungry that I ate two _____ for lunch!
4 Some of the best-selling _____ in our shop are flat-screen TVs, laptops and mobile handsets.
5 The world's first _____ was not Google, but Archie, and it appeared in 1990.

2 Read the definitions. Then complete the words by adding the missing vowels.

1 things like belts and jewellery, which look nice with your clothes: _cc_ss_r_ _s
2 the full form of email: _l_ctr_n_c_ m_ _l
3 clothes for football, tennis, basketball, etc: sp_rtsw_ _r
4 shoes for running: tr_ _n_rs
5 sweet cakes: p_str_ _s

Grammar focus 1
Present simple passive

3 Complete the passive sentences with the correct form of the verb *to be*.

1 The internet __is__ used by millions of people every day.
2 _____ students taught German at this school?
3 In my town, about 15 babies _____ born each week.
4 What _____ your sister called?
5 Approximately 1,000 films _____ made each year in India.
6 Coffee _____ grown in Brazil.
7 Where _____ the Telugu language spoken?
8 _____ dogs usually allowed in restaurants in your country?

4 Complete the sentences with the Present simple passive form of the verbs in brackets.

1 71 percent of the world __is covered__ (cover) by water.
2 The word *the* _____ (use) 63,924 times in the Bible.
3 6,000 postmen _____ (bite) by British dogs every year.
4 2,019 cars _____ (steal) in the United States every day.
5 112 different languages _____ (speak) in the Russian Federation.
6 About 300,000,000 photocopies _____ (make) in Europe every day.
7 In a normal year, five people _____ (kill) by lightning in England and Wales.
8 2.4 litres of water _____ (lose) by the human body every day.

5 Put the words in the correct order to make questions.

cotton   to see in the dark   over your eyes   every day
~~in supermarkets and pharmacies~~   in Brazil and Portugal
with a special ball called 'a softball'   to stop it melting
8:30 p.m.   water, sugar and a secret ingredient
to mobile phones   with *be* and the past participle

1 is / sold / Where / shampoo?
   A: *Where is shampoo sold?*
   B: *In supermarkets and pharmacies.*
2 spoken / Portuguese / is / Where?
   A: _____
   B: _____
3 made / cola / What / of / is?
   A: _____
   B: _____
4 are / sent / Where / text messages?
   A: _____
   B: _____
5 freezer / is / Why / ice cream / a / kept / in?
   A: _____
   B: _____
6 used / What / for / torch / a / is?
   A: _____
   B: _____
7 sunglasses / worn / usually / are / Where?
   A: _____
   B: _____
8 is / passive / made / the / How?
   A: _____
   B: _____
9 often / the / is / How / office / cleaned?
   A: _____
   B: _____
10 dinner / What / is / time / served / usually?
   A: _____
   B: _____
11 these / are / made / shirts / of / What?
   A: _____
   B: _____
12 played / is / how / sport / this?
   A: _____
   B: _____

Pronunciation
Regular past participles

6a Look at the list of past participles. How many syllables do they have? Complete the table.

~~appeared~~   ~~considered~~   created   helped   increased
looked   loved   needed   proved   received   represented
supported

1 syllable	2 syllables	3 syllables	4 syllables
	appeared	*considered*	

b 🎧 **12.1** Listen and check.

c Three of the past participles in exercise a are pronounced /t/. Which three?

d Listen again and check.

Vocabulary
Personal items

7 Choose the correct answers.

1 Which one does a woman use?
   perfume / aftershave
2 Which is it easier to keep in your pocket?
   comb / hairbrush
3 What does a man shave with?
   razor and shaving foam / aftershave
4 Where can you wear a bracelet?
   on your neck / around your wrist
5 What do people usually put under their arms?
   deodorant / perfume
6 Where can you wear a necklace?
   on your finger / around your neck
7 Which one is a piece of jewellery?
   earring / moisturiser
8 Which one does a woman use on her face?
   nail varnish / eyeliner

Grammar focus 2
Past simple passive

8 Complete the biography of the designer Gianni Versace with the Past simple passive form of the verbs in brackets.

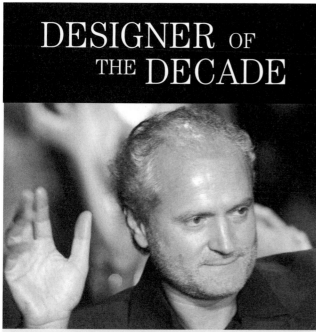

DESIGNER OF THE DECADE

Italian Gianni Versace was one of the best-known fashion designers of the 20th century. Sometimes his clothes ¹ _were criticised_ (criticise), but they ² _____ (buy) by the rich and famous – particularly people from the worlds of pop music and film.

Versace came from Calabria, in the south of Italy, where his mother was a dressmaker. He moved to the northern city of Milan in the 1970s, and his first collection ³ _____ (launch) in 1978. Soon, his brother Santo and his sister Donatella ⁴ _____ (give) jobs in the growing Versace empire. He bought homes in Milan, Paris, New York and Miami, which ⁵ _____ (fill) with works of art from all over the world. In 1994, the English actress Elizabeth Hurley wore a Versace dress on the first night of the film *Four Weddings and a Funeral* in London. The simple black dress, which ⁶ _____ (hold) together by a few safety pins, was a sensation. The next day, the photos ⁷ _____ (see) all over the world and from that moment, the name Versace ⁸ _____ (know) everywhere. His clothes ⁹ _____ (wear) by superstars such as Elton John, Madonna, Courtney Love, Princess Diana and the supermodel Naomi Campbell.

Versace ¹⁰ _____ (murder) on 15th July 1997 outside his home in Miami Beach. His memorial service in Milan Cathedral ¹¹ _____ (attend) by 2,000 people. Millions watched on television as a tearful Elton John ¹² _____ (comfort) by Princess Diana, who herself died tragically just a few weeks later.

9a Each sentence contains one grammar mistake. Correct the mistakes.

1 Lipstick were invented in Iraq.
   Lipstick was invented in Iraq.
2 Electric razors were introduce in the 1930s.
   _____

3 Milk chocolate be first sold in the 1870s.
   _____

4 The first email is sent in 1991.
   _____

5 426 million dollars were spend on jewellery in the world in 2010.
   _____

6 In Ancient Egypt, the metals copper and lead was used to make eyeliner.
   _____

7 The world's first MP3 player was produce in 1997 in Korea.
   _____

8 More than 30 million i-pads were sell in 2011.
   _____

9 The first wallpaper was print in France in the 18th century.
   _____

10 The vacuum cleaner were invented by a cleaner who became ill every time he cleaned a floor.
   _____

b There is one piece of incorrect information in exercise a. The other nine pieces of information are correct. Which sentence do you think is incorrect?

Grammar focus 1

Present perfect continuous with *how long*, *for* and *since*

3 Write one sentence using the Present perfect continuous for each pair of pictures.

1 *She has been working in the office for two hours.*
(work)

2 _____ (rain)

3 _____ (play tennis)

4 _____ (walk)

4 Complete the time phrases with *for* or *since*.

1 ___*for*___ a week
2 ___*since*___ 2011
3 _____ 20 minutes
4 _____ he was born
5 _____ Thursday
6 _____ then
7 _____ last week
8 _____ 9 o'clock
9 _____ this morning
10 _____ you left school
11 _____ six months
12 _____ an hour
13 _____ 20 years

5a Choose one of the phrases from exercise 4 to complete each sentence in a logical way.

1 Today's the last day of our holiday. We've been here
___*for a week*___ .

2 She left home two days ago and no one has seen her _____ .

3 You probably haven't studied mathematics
_____ .

4 I've been driving _____ and I've never had an accident!

5 South Sudan has been an independent country
_____ .

6 I'm so hungry! I haven't eaten anything
_____ .

7 Excuse me, waitress, is our meal coming? We've been waiting _____ !

8 I'm not surprised you're tired – you haven't slept
_____ .

b 🎧 **13.2** Listen and check.

6 Read the article and use the prompts below to write questions about it.
Then write answers with *for* or *since*.

Success from abroad

Thomas Eckhardt: Thomas came to London from Germany almost four years ago. After doing a course in theatre costume design, he began working at the National Theatre in London a year ago. 'I really enjoy designing clothes and I've always loved the theatre, so this job is absolutely perfect for me,' he says. 'I started work on a new production of *Romeo and Juliet* two weeks ago and I'm really excited about it.'

Bianca and Richard Jones: Bianca Jones is originally from Lima, Peru. She came to England in 2007 and a year later she got married. For the last two years, she has been manager of La Finca restaurant with her English husband, Richard. 'We were London's only Peruvian restaurant. It's been so successful that last week we opened a new restaurant – La Finca II.'

Kerry Paterson: When Kerry first came to England from Australia in 2005, she was a backpacker, travelling round Europe. She came back three years later and started working as a swimming coach about a year after that. Nowadays, she has a second, part-time job: playing in a jazz band. 'About a month ago, a friend heard that I could play the piano and asked me to join his band. We play every weekend in local cafés and restaurants.'

1 how long / Thomas / live / in England?
A: *How long has Thomas been living in England?*
B: *For four years.*

2 how long / he / work / at the National Theatre?
A: _____
B: _____

3 how long / he / work / on *Romeo and Juliet*?
A: _____
B: _____

4 how long / Bianca / live / in England?
A: _____
B: _____

5 how long / she / work / at La Finca?
A: _____
B: _____

6 how long / La Finca II / operate?
A: _____
B: _____

7 how long / Kerry / live / in England?
A: _____
B: _____

8 how long / she / work / as a swimming coach?
A: _____
B: _____

Pronunciation

Contracted forms

7 🎧 **13.3 Listen and tick (✓) the sentence you hear.**

1 **a** I have been working very hard. ✓
  b I've been working very hard. ☐
2 **a** She has been going out a lot recently. ☐
  b She's been going out a lot recently. ☐
3 **a** My brother has been applying for jobs. ☐
  b My brother's been applying for jobs. ☐
4 **a** What have you been doing? ☐
  b What've you been doing? ☐
5 **a** They have been staying with me for a week. ☐
  b They've been staying with me for a week. ☐
6 **a** What has been happening? ☐
  b What's been happening? ☐

Grammar focus 2

Present perfect continuous and Present perfect simple

8 **Tick the five correct sentences. Correct the mistakes in five of the sentences.**

1 I've been working for about three hours. ✓

2 I've been having this watch for over 20 years. ☐
  I've had this watch for over 20 years.

3 The President has been talking for nearly an hour. ☐

4 How long have you been waiting? ☐

5 I've been liking chocolate for years. ☐

6 Have you been knowing Sylvia for a long time? ☐

7 She's been reading that book for weeks. ☐

8 I haven't been seeing Michael for years and years. ☐

9 I've been hating spinach since I was a child. ☐

10 Katerina has been staying with her grandmother for the last two weeks. ☐

9 **Choose the correct answers.**

1 I think **I've met** / I've been meeting the man who I'm going to marry!
2 **I've read** / **I've been reading** this novel and I really want to know what happens in the end.
3 Ann **has been looking** / **has looked** for a job for three months, and she still **hasn't been finding** / **hasn't found** one.
4 **They've been building** / **They've built** their house for ages and they hope to finish next year.
5 **I've got** / **I've been getting** new qualifications all my life.
6 **I've been starting** / **I've started** a new job with a good salary.
7 Have you **been filling in** / **filled in** the application form yet?
8 She's always **been loving** / **loved** animals.

Vocabulary

Getting a job

10 **Complete the text by writing the words in the box in the correct place.**

agency   on   in   ~~for~~   a   details   been   time

> *for*
> I've been looking ʌ a job since October. I've written CV with
> all my qualifications and personal so people can contact me.
> I log to job websites every day, fill all the application forms
> and send them my CV. But I haven't for an interview yet.
> My brother has started working in a recruitment, so I hope
> he'll help me find a nice part- job.

Vocabulary
Money

1 Choose the correct answers.

1 He's lost his *wallet* / *credit card* – it's got his keys in, and 70 euros in bank notes.
2 When you buy something, always keep the *coins* / *receipt*. You might need to take it back to the shop.
3 Excuse me, where's the nearest *exchange rate* / *cashpoint*, please?
4 I didn't buy any *foreign currency* / *change* because the exchange rate wasn't very good.
5 I buy things with my *bank notes* / *credit card* more often than with cash.
6 The restaurant was great, but the waiter made a mistake with our *bill* / *purse*.

Pronunciation
Numbers

2a How do we say these numbers? Choose a or b.

1 600
  a six hundreds   **b** six hundred
2 14.5
  a fourteen point five   b fourteen comma five
3 124
  a one hundred twenty-four
  b one hundred and twenty-four
4 $99
  a ninety-nine dollars   b dollars ninety-nine
5 (the year) 1996
  a nineteen ninety-six
  b one thousand nine hundred and ninety-six
6 £370,000
  a three hundred and seventy thousands pounds
  b three hundred and seventy thousand pounds

b 🎧 **14.1** Listen and check.

Grammar focus 1
Past perfect

3a Complete the sentences with the Past perfect form of the verbs in brackets.

1 Nadia said she was very sorry for what she
   had done (do).
2 When Sam _____ (pay) the bill, we left the restaurant and went home.
3 It wasn't surprising that she was tired – she _____ (not sleep) for two days.
4 The road was blocked because a lorry _____ (break down).
5 During the afternoon, David spent all the money he _____ (win) in the morning.
6 My mother felt very nervous on the plane because she _____ (not fly) before.
7 When the police arrived to arrest him, Thompson _____ (leave).
8 _____ (they / go) home when you arrived?
9 I _____ (hear) the story before, so I didn't find it very interesting.
10 After she _____ (try on) all the dresses in the shop, she bought the most expensive one.
11 They _____ (not have) breakfast when I got up.
12 The children were very excited because they _____ (not see) a tiger before.

b 🎧 **14.2** Listen and check.

Grammar focus 2
Narrative tenses review

8 Choose the correct answers.

1 The show had already **began** / **begun** when we got to the stadium.
2 It was a marvellous show and Maria **sang** / **sung** beautifully.
3 I was very tired because I had **drove** / **driven** all the way from Warsaw to Vienna.
4 While I was swimming in the sea, someone **stole** / **stolen** my clothes.
5 When she died in 1999, the novelist Iris Murdoch had **wrote** / **written** 27 novels.
6 The X-rays showed that Laurence had **broke** / **broken** his leg.
7 I had never **saw** / **seen** anything so beautiful in my whole life.
8 When we got home, the children had **fell** / **fallen** asleep in the car.

9 Complete the sentences with the Past simple, Past continuous or Past perfect form of the verbs in brackets.

1 They _had already got_ (already / get) married when we met them.
2 I got up, _____ (have) breakfast and left.
3 It was a beautiful morning. The sun was shining and the birds _____ (sing).
4 I was sure I _____ (see) him somewhere before, but I couldn't remember where.
5 She walked out of her flat. As she shut the door, she realised she _____ (forget) the key.
6 My leg started to hurt while I _____ (play) hockey.
7 I grew up in Haiti and I _____ (live) in New York for a few years in the 1990s.
8 When I was a child, I didn't know what job I _____ (want) to do in the future.
9 The fire alarm went off when we _____ (have) a French lesson.
10 He _____ (work) when I called him this morning.

10a Put the sentences in the correct order. Write the full story in the space on the right.

a no one in the driver's seat. But someone had ☐
b say 'yes'? I hope she did! ☐
c written a message on the side of the van. It ☐
d marry me?' I suppose this man and his girlfriend, Linda, ☐
e gone. I'd love to know what happened in the end; did Linda ☐
f I was driving to work yesterday morning when ☐1
g said, 'Linda, I'm sorry. I love you with all my heart. Will you ☐
h I noticed a white van parked by the road. There was ☐
i going to work again this morning, the van had ☐
j had had an argument. Perhaps Linda had ☐
k told him she didn't want to see him again? Anyway, when I was ☐

I was driving to work yesterday morning when _____
_____
_____
_____
_____
_____
_____
_____
_____
_____
_____
_____
_____
_____

b Find all the examples of the Past simple, Past continuous and Past perfect in the story in exercise a.

11 Tick the correct sentence.

1a While Jeremy had a shower, his dog had eaten his steak. ☐

b While Jeremy was having a shower, his dog ate his steak. ✓

2a All the guests left by the time we had arrived at the party. ☐

b All the guests had left by the time we arrived at the party. ☐

3a When I got back to the car park, I saw that someone had stolen my car. ☐

b When I had got back to the car park, I saw that someone stole my car. ☐

4a She was reading a book when she fell asleep. ☐

b She had read a book when she was falling asleep. ☐

5a When the exam was finishing, I knew I did really well. ☐

b When the exam finished, I knew I had done really well. ☐

6a I decided to sell my bike because I hadn't used it for a year. ☐

b I was deciding to sell my bike because I didn't use it for a year. ☐

7a The restaurant was noisy because several young children were crying. ☐

b The restaurant had been noisy because several young children cried. ☐

8a My camera had broken after I was only having it for a week. ☐

b My camera broke after I'd only had it for a week. ☐

9a He was working when I left. ☐

b He was working when I'd left. ☐

10a They already went to bed when we had got back. ☐

b They'd already gone to bed when we got back. ☐

Language live
Dealing with money

12a Put the words in the correct order.

1 £10 / Could / lend / you / me?

2 have / Can / the / please / bill, / we?

3 How / you / do / I / owe / much?

4 Do / a / you / we / leave / tip / should / think?

5 got / Have / you / a / €20 / change / for / note?

b Match the questions from exercise a with replies a–e.

a It's £46.20, please. ☐

b Let me see. Yes, I've got two tens. ☐

c Well, OK. But can you pay me back tomorrow? ☐

d No, I don't think we should. The food wasn't very good. ☐

e Certainly. I'll bring it to you now. I hope you enjoyed your meal. ☐

c 🎧 **14.4** Listen and check.

Writing
An essay expressing your opinion

13a Fabio's teacher has given him this homework task: *Is it better to buy things on the internet or to buy them in a shop? Write an essay giving your answer.* Look at Fabio's answer and the phrases in bold. One word is wrong in each phrase. Find the incorrect word and replace it with the right word from the box.

both   In   say   ~~it~~   other   For   one

it
Online shopping is getting more and more popular. But is ~~this~~ true to say that it's better than buying things in shops? It's a difficult question and **there are arguments on every sides**.

On a hand, internet shopping is usually cheaper. **People often tell that** you should buy things from the cheapest place. So if the cheapest place is an online shop, that's where they buy from. Doing this can save you time as well as money because you don't have to leave your home.

On the second hand, when online shops do more business, traditional shops do less business. Lots of shops have closed in my town; and it's happening everywhere. It's really sad and I think it's happening because of internet shopping. **With me**, going to a shop and speaking to the shop assistant helps me decide what to buy.

At my opinion, online shopping might be cheaper and quicker. But it certainly isn't better than going to a traditional shop, where you get good customer service.

b 🎧 **14.5** Listen and check.

c Now write an essay giving your opinion on one of these subjects.

1 Do sports stars earn too much money?
2 What is more important in life than money?
3 Is it better to spend or to save?

Answer key

12 a
1 so
2 because
3 but
4 then
5 and

UNIT 3

1 a
2 asleep
3 nap
4 a shower
5 to eat
6 energetic
7 up
8 home
9 to bed
10 work

b
1 finish work
2 feel energetic
3 have a shower
4 have something to eat
5 go to bed
6 fall asleep
7 wake up
8 get up
9 have a nap
10 relax at home

2 (NB: Some answers may be different in different cultures.)
2 should
3 shouldn't
4 shouldn't
5 shouldn't
6 shouldn't
7 should
8 should

3
2 d
3 b
4 e
5 g
6 a
7 c

4 b
1 e
2 a
3 b

c
1 Pietro
2 Darek
3 Darek
4 Amy
5 Pietro
6 Amy

5 a
2 My sister can speak three languages perfectly.
3 I can't do this exercise!
4 Now you can buy cheap plane tickets on the internet.
5 Renate can't come to the party.
6 Can you read French? I don't understand this.
7 We can't answer the phone at the moment.
8 Can we sit by the window?
9 Only students can use the library.
10 You can't come in here.

6 a
2 have to find
3 don't have to do
4 have to write
5 don't have to wear
6 have to wear
7 don't have to answer
8 have to try
9 don't have to worry
10 don't have to worry
11 have to be

7
2 Can
3 can't
4 don't have to
5 have to
6 can
7 Can
8 can't
9 have to
10 has to
11 can
12 Can
13 have to
14 can't

8 a
1 can't
2 can't
3 can
4 can
5 can't

b
2 a
3 b
4 b
5 b
6 a
7 b
8 a
9 b
10 b

9
1 CHEF
2 PLUMBER
3 DRIVER
4 ACCOUNTANT
5 NANNY
6 JUDGE
7 TRANSLATOR

UNIT 4

1 a

Ooo	O	Oo	oO	oOo
January	March	April	July	*September*
February	May	August		October
	June			November
				December

b
2 ð
3 ð, θ
4 ð, θ
5 ð, θ, θ
6 ð, θ

2 a
2 out
3 off
4 prepare
5 invited
6 exchanged
7 making
8 up
9 relatives
10 buys

b
2 send
3 visit
4 prepared
5 invited
6 had
7 buy
8 make
9 eat
10 exchange

3
2 am I driving, you are
3 are you doing, am not watching
4 looking for, Are you sitting
5 isn't working, is spending
6 are you going, are waiting
7 Are you talking, I am, aren't listening
8 is that man looking, isn't looking, is sitting

4
2 are you doing
3 you're listening
4 are you writing
5 Do you eat
6 are you laughing
7 Does your brother play
8 Are you listening

5
3 ✗ I don't believe you!
4 ✓
5 ✗ I don't understand this exercise.
6 ✗ I hate cold weather.
7 ✓

6
2 don't want
3 loves
4 is studying
5 understand
6 isn't working
7 don't have
8 are you reading

7 a
2 tasty
3 noisy
4 delicious
5 peaceful
6 delicious

b
1 b
2 c
3 a
4 e
5 d

c
2 friendly
3 exciting
4 spicy
5 delicious
6 boiling
7 noisy
8 peaceful

8
2 am not going
3 Are you coming
4 are flying
5 is driving
6 are you doing
7 are coming back
8 are you going
9 isn't staying
10 Is your dad working

9 a
Suggested answers:
Steve isn't working on Monday.
He's playing squash with Andy at 10:30.
He's going to Manchester for the day on Tuesday.
He's catching the train at 6:45.
Judy's working on Monday and Wednesday.
She's meeting Alison for lunch on Friday at one o'clock.
Steve and Judy are going to the cinema on Thursday.
Steve's mum is coming to babysit.
Oliver's playing football on Tuesday at four o'clock.
He's going to Tom's house on Wednesday after school.
Florence is going swimming on Monday.
Oliver and Florence are meeting their cousins in the park at 2:30 on Friday.
The whole family is having lunch with the grandparents at twelve o'clock on Sunday.

10 a
2 Are you having a day off this week?
3 What are you doing next weekend?
4 Are your relatives coming to visit in the near future?
5 When are you having your next English lesson?
6 Are you meeting your friends later today?
7 Who's cooking dinner in your house this evening?
8 Is anyone in you family going to the dentist this month?

b
Students' own answers

11 a
1 I hope you'll be very happy
2 Many happy returns
3 Thanks for inviting me.
4 Happy New Year
5 Safe journey!

12 a
2 g
3 c
4 k
5 e
6 b
8 d
9 a
10 i
11 l
12 j

Pearson Education Limited
Edinburgh Gate
Harlow
Essex CM20 2JE
England
and Associated Companies throughout the world.

www.pearsonelt.com

First published 2013
Sixth impression 2018

ISBN: 978-1-4479-0663-6

Set in 10.5pt Bless Light
Printed in Italy by L.E.G.O. S.p.A. Lavis (TN)

Photo acknowledgements
*The publisher would like to thank the following for their kind permission
to reproduce their photographs:*

(Key: b-bottom; c-centre; l-left; r-right; t-top)

Alamy Images: Arcaid Images 44c, DBURKE 54l, MBI 18 (6),
Old Visuals 9, Paris Cafe 17b, Radius Images 54r, Stockbroker 29,
SuperStock. Ingram Publishing 16; **Corbis:** 62l, Julian Calder 72tl, Jens
Kalaene / dpa 36l, Sunset Boulevard 26, Tanya Constantine / Blend
Images 37t, Tetra Images 45; **Fotolia.com:** 3darcastudio 48, Yuri Arcurs
30, artphaneuf 18 (5), AZP Worldwide 67c, Balloge 21l, Brilt 39 (b),
Kevin Eaves 21r, Elnur 63br, Frog 974 57r, goodluz 18 (2), Maksym
Gorpenyuk 38t, grahammoore999 47b, Chris Hill 60l, jojjik 71b, Robert
Kneschke 12, lightpoet 13tl, Lokalin 55, Pavel Losevsky 39 (c), Yahia
Loukkal 63tl, mangostock 67t, markus_marb 39 (e), michaeljung 18
(3), micromonkey 19, Monkey Business 4bl, nyul 67b, 68, 72r, ollirg
11bl, Perseomedusa 69t, Andres Rodriguez 71t, ryanking999 18 (4),
Mihaly Samu 40bl, Maria Sbytova 18 (1), sfmthd 22, TheSupe87
37b, Graça Victoria 63bc; **Getty Images:** AFP 34t, 61l, Howard Grey
50l, Ryan McVay 17t, Darren Robb 5; **Imagemore Co., Ltd:** 69b;
NASA: 46; **Pearson Education Ltd:** Sophie Bluy 27, Jules Selmes
15b; **Photoshot Holdings Limited:** UPPA 38b; **Press Association
Images:** AP 34b; **Reuters:** Goran Tomasevic 40br; **Rex Features:**
David Crump / Daily Mail 24t, FremantleMedia Ltd 6l, Julian Makey
24b, Moviestore Collection 6c, 11br, PictureGroup 6r; **Shutterstock.
com:** 2009fotofriends 53t, 89studio 60r, Alinochka 39 (f), Andresr 53b,
auremar 8bl, Andre Blais 47t, Blend Images 18 (7), Igor Borodin 28,
Collpicto 33b, Matthew Connolly 59r, Ian D Walker 33t, eurobanks 15c,
GoldPixelStudio 63tc, Goodluz 52b, J. Helgason 56r, hfng 50c, iofoto
14, javarman 39 (a), Ruslan Kudrin 65r, Andrew Lever 15t, David P
Lewis 39br, Losevsky Photo and Video 52t, lucadp 39 (d), ostill 62r,
Sergey Peterman 66, privilege 20, Alexander Raths 13tr, Luis Santos
65l, Pablo Scapinachis 57l, shutswis 44b, 63bl, stefanolunardi 8br,
StockLite 50r, 56l, tavi 63tr, Joao Virissimo 59l, Tracy Whiteside 65c,
wrangler 58; **Sozaijiten:** 36r; **SuperStock:** Fine Art Images 34c, Robert
Harding Picture Library 4br; **Veer/Corbis:** rsinha 44t

Cover images: *Front:* **PhotoDisc:** Siede Preis Photography

All other images © Pearson Education

In some instances we have been unable to trace the owners of copyright
material, and we would appreciate any information that would enable us
to do so.

Illustrated by Colin Brown, Kes Hankin (Gemini Design), Andy
Hammond, Connie Jude, Tim Kahane, Julian Mosedale, Chris Pavely,
Theresa Tibberts, Mark Vallance (Gemini Design)